First Baptist Church
PLYMOUTH 8 INDIANA
GOSHEN, INDIANA 46526

DISCIPLESHIP

Growing Up As a Christian

DISCIPLESHIP
Growing Up As a Christian

G. Campbell Morgan

KREGEL PUBLICATIONS
Grand Rapids, Michigan 49501

Discipleship: Growing Up As a Christian by
G. Campbell Morgan. © 1991 by Kregel Publications,
a division of Kregel, Inc. P. O. Box 2607, Grand Rapids,
MI 49501. All rights reserved. No portion of this book
may be reproduced in any form without the written
permission of the publishers, except for brief quotations
in magazine reviews, etc.
Unless otherwise indicated, all scripture references are
from the New International Version, copyright © 1978
by the International Bible Society. Used by permission
of the Zondervan Corporation.

Cover Photo: COMSTOCK INC.
Cover and Book Design: Al Hartman

Library of Congress Cataloging in Publication Data

Morgan, G. Campbell (George Campbell), 1863-1945
   Discipleship: growing up as a Christian / G. Campbell
Morgan.
       p.   cm.
   Reprint, with new introduction. Originally published: F. H.
Revell, 1897.

   1. Christian Life.   I. Title.

BV4501.M7655   1991   248.4—dc20   91-15196
                                          CIP
   ISBN 0-8254-3259-6 (pbk.)

         1 2 3 4 5 Printing/Year 94 93 92 91

         Printed in the United States of America

DEDICATION

To my wife in whose unobtrusive and consistent discipleship I have found the inspiration of service, and that sense of "sanctuary" in the home which has been largely the strength of service also, I dedicate this, my first book.

CONTENTS

Publisher's Preface

Discipleship was the first book written by G. Campbell Morgan, and it is noteworthy for its strongly biblical content and practical application so characteristic of all his writings. Some sixty books and eleven pamphlets came from Morgan's gifted and prolific pen, as well as *The Analyzed Bible* published in 1964. Morgan was a powerful and unique Bible preacher, born and educated in England. As was so often the case with English public speakers, he was a powerful and incisive verbal communicator. His written work was characterized by that same quality.

G. Campbell Morgan had an active and productive ministry. Ordained in 1889, he pastored in both England and America, spoke at the popular Northfield Bible Conference, and traveled widely preaching and lecturing.

Born in a Gloucestershire village, he was the son of a Baptist minister who had resigned his pastorate to start a faith mission. Morgan was reared in a religious atmosphere and preached his first sermon at the age of thirteen. Without academic training, he joined the staff of a Jewish school, learning a great deal from the headmaster, a Rabbi. After he was rejected for ordination by both the Salvation Army and the Methodists, he was accepted by the Congregationalists as a full-time minister and went on to pastor many churches, including his most famous, Westminster Chapel, London (1904-1917 and 1933-1945). He was president of Cheshunt College, Cambridge, from 1911 to 1914. His travels took place especially from 1919 to 1932. His preaching and skill at Bible expositions attracted great crowds and resulted in many conversions.

Thousands came to hear Morgan preach and teach the Scriptures. The main purpose of his exemplary life was to make the Bible clear and applicable to everyday experience. He accomplished that aim to a remarkable degree.

G. Campbell Morgan was a keen student of the Bible, as well as other disciplines. That gift was the key to his charm and attractiveness as a preacher. He was always learning, consistently coming up with new and incisive insights. All who read his books or heard him preach were the richer for the experience. He consistently delved deeper and deeper into the Greek and English texts of the Scriptures.

But one guiding principle underlay his discoveries and the exciting observations he shared. That discovery was what he called the "contextual principle" of Bible interpretation. By the term he simply meant that a passage must always be viewed in the light of its context, both immediate and broader. Scripture best interprets Scripture, said Morgan. An isolated text is not really an entity in itself: it is part of a complete literary unit, and that unit is in turn part of a larger one. Eventually the text must be seen as part of the whole of Scripture.

This emphasis on the contextual principle protected Morgan from unwise interpretations, inevitable when one tries to explain a text out of context. Morgan once illustrated this in a humorous way when he explained how he had been cured of frivolous attempts to interpret the Bible. Looking for guidance, he flipped open the pages at random and ran his finger down the column. He was pointing to the story of Balaam and his ass! Another time he showed how choosing isolated "proof texts" could prove just about anything. For example, he said he could prove that his audience should go out and hang themselves because Judas "went and hanged himself" (Matthew 27:5) and Luke 10:37 says, "Go, and do thou likewise."

Because he was unable to attend school in his early years, he enjoyed the privilege of study with an excellent tutor at home. This grounded him in solid learning. His father's involvement in preaching instilled in the young Morgan a love for the Scriptures. In addition, the death of his sister also served to increase the young boy's sensitivity to the hurts of others. Even as a boy he was adept at self-examination and learned how to apply his insights to people in difficult or tragic circumstances.

Probably the most important event of Morgan's life as a preacher was a period of some two or three years before his twenty-first birthday. During that time he questioned and searched his own faith. Reflecting on that, Morgan calls it the time his "early faith passed under eclipse." He even quit preaching and refused to open his Bible for two years, which he called the "two years of sadness and sorrow." During that time he experimented with one philosophy after another, but none met his need. Finally, he took all of his books, with their theories and notions, and locked them away in a cupboard for seven long years. Then he bought a new Bible and began to read it alone with an open and searching mind, and a will determined to discover God's message to him. The Bible made his heart glow, and the Word calmed his troubled intellect. He wrote that the Scriptures gave him that "satisfaction that I had sought for elsewhere." From that time on, Morgan lived to preach the Bible.

Thousands enjoyed his ministry at Westminster Chapel in London. People flocked there to hear him, and when he came to the United States, he met the same kind of response.

The well-known Bible teacher, Wilbur M. Smith, testified that though he had been moved by many speakers, no one could cast a spell over an audience as could G. Campbell Morgan.

Perhaps John Henry Jowett singled out the key to Morgan's effectiveness when he noted that he let the Bible tell its own message. Morgan's genius for communicating that message was incomparable.

Dr. Warren W. Wiersbe says of George Campbell Morgan, "He had no formal training for the ministry, but his tireless devotion to the study of the Bible helped him to become one of the leading Bible teachers of his day. Rejected by the Methodists, he was ordained into the Congregational ministry. He was associated with Dwight L. Moody in the Northfield Bible Conference and as an itinerant Bible teacher. He is best known as the pastor of Westminster Chapel, London. During his second term there, he had Dr. D. Martyn Lloyd-Jones as his associate."

Kregel Publications is privileged to make Morgan's almost forgotten book on *Discipleship* again available to a new audience of younger readers, many of them unfamiliar with the riches available from the brilliant mind and incisive pen of a pulpit master of a past generation.

FOREWORD

This book is not intended to be a deeply theological work, nor is it addressed to theologians as such, not that they or their work is undervalued. They of varied schools have placed the writer under a debt to them that he is unable to repay.

Along practical lines, it is intended to be an aid to the disciples of Jesus. I have tried to show, in some measure at least, the eminent practicality of the Christian life. Power to live this life is communicated by and sustained in Christ through the Holy Spirit.

It is further intended to reveal the actual effect of this power on this present life, ennobling it in all its relationships, and filling it with all joy and beauty. This is the ultimate intention of the Master for all His disciples.

To the glory of God, and the help of fellow-disciples, it is therefore prayerfully sent forth on its mission.

G. CAMPBELL MORGAN

New Court Congregational Church,
London 1897

1

The dullest natural intellect may be—
and *is*—rendered keen and receptive
Godward, by the incoming of the Holy
Spirit.

At the feet of Jesus
Is the place for me,
There, a humble learner,
Would I choose to be.
—Philip P. Bliss

BECOMING A DISCIPLE

The word, "disciple," is the term consistently used in the four
Gospels to mark the relationship existing between Christ and
His followers. Jesus used it Himself in speaking of them, and
they in speaking of each other. Neither did it pass out of use in
the new days of Pentecostal power. It runs right through the
Acts of the Apostles. It is also interesting to remember that the
angels thought and spoke of these men as "disciples." The use of
the word in the days of the Incarnation is linked to the use of the

word in the apostolic age by the angelic message to the women, "Go, tell his *disciples* and Peter" (Mark 16:7).

It is somewhat remarkable that the word is not to be found in the Epistles. This is to be accounted for by the fact that the Epistles were addressed to Christians in their corporate capacity as churches, and so spoke of them as members of such, and as the "saints" or separated ones of God. The term disciple marks an *individual* relationship. It is of the utmost value to mark the relationship existing between Christ and each single soul. As such, it is useful as a suggestion of our consequent position in all the varied circumstances of everyday living. Let us look now at . . .

What It Means

The word "disciple" itself signifies "a taught or trained one," and gives us the ideal of relationship. Jesus is the Teacher. He has all knowledge of the ultimate purposes of God for man, of the will of God concerning man, of the laws of God that mark for man the path of his progress and final crowning. Disciples are those who gather around this Teacher and are trained by Him. These seekers after truth, not merely in the abstract, but as a life force, come to Him and join the circle of those to whom He reveals these great secrets of all true life. Sitting at His feet, they learn from the unfolding of His lessons the will and ways of God for them. Obeying each successive word, they realize, within themselves, the renewing force and uplifting power of a vital relationship with Him. The true and perpetual condition of discipleship, and its ultimate issue, were clearly declared by the Lord Himself "to those Jews who believed him." "If you hold to my teaching, you are really my disciples. Then you will know the truth, and the truth will set you free" (John 8:31, 32). Before considering the glorious enduement the Teacher confers on every disciple, and the stringent requirements that guard the entrance to discipleship, it is very important that we should have clearly outlined in our minds the true meaning of this phase of the relationship, which Jesus bears to His people.

This relationship is not that of a *lecturer,* from whose messages men may or may not deduce applications for themselves. It is not that of a *prophet* merely, making a private pronouncement, and leaving the issues of the same. It certainly is not that of a *specialist* on a given subject, declaring his knowledge, to the interest of a few, the amazement of more, and the bewilderment of most. No, it is none of these.

It is that of a *teacher*—Himself possessing full knowledge—bending over a pupil, and for a set purpose, with an end in view, imparting knowledge step by step, point by point, ever moving toward a definite end. That conception includes also the true ideal of our position. We are not casual *listeners,* neither are we merely interested *hearers* desiring information. Rather, we are *disciples,* looking toward and desiring the same end as the Master, and therefore listening to every word, marking every inflection of His voice that carries meaning—and applying all our energy to realizing the Teacher's purpose for us. Such is the ideal.

What It Involves

Now let us consider the privileges the Teacher confers upon those who become His disciples.

The first is the establishment of a relationship that makes it possible *for Him to teach and for us to be taught.* The question of sin must be dealt with, and also that which results from sin—our inability to understand the teaching. Christ never becomes a teacher to those who are living in sin. Sin, as actual transgression in the past, must be pardoned. And sin, as a principle of revolution within, must be cleansed. So before He unfolds one word of the divine law of life, or reveals in any particular the line of progress, He deals with this twofold aspect of sin.

To the soul judging past sin by confessing it and turning from it, He dispenses *forgiveness,* pronouncing His priestly absolution by virtue of His own atonement on the Cross. To the soul yielded to Him absolutely and unreservedly, one who consents to the death of self, He gives the blessing of *cleansing* from sin.

By this statement of His dealing with us I do not insist on an order of procedure from pardon to cleansing. It is, rather, the declaration of the twofold aspect of the first work of Christ for His disciples, the bestowment of the initial blessing. In practical experience, men usually, though not invariably, and not necessarily, realize the first-named first in order. This is the result of the overwhelming and largely selfish desire of personal safety, a desire that is natural and proper following the divinely imparted instinct of self-preservation. Nevertheless, they should at once, for the higher reason of God's glory, seek to realize the deeper side of the one blessing, that of cleansing.

Our Father's patience is manifested, however, in the midst of our folly. He forgives and graciously waits. When we look at Him again and say, "Master, there is more in Your cross than pardon," then He makes us conscious of His power to cleanse. It is certain that there can be no real discipleship apart from the realization of the twofold blessing. Beyond this there lies the dullness of our understanding, our inability to comprehend the truths He declares. This He overcomes by the gift of the Holy Spirit, who makes clear to us the teaching of the Master. What a priceless gift this is. The dullest intellect may be—and is—rendered keen and receptive Godward, by the Holy Spirit.

So He Himself provides for, and creates, the relationships of *communion* through cleansing, and *intelligence* through the indwelling of the Spirit. These constitute our condition for receiving what He has to teach.

Proving by Practice

The other great privilege to be remembered is that the school of Jesus is a technical one. He provides opportunities for us to prove, in practical life, the truths He has declared. It is a great essential in His method with which we shall deal more fully in a subsequent chapter. Another evidence of His abounding grace is this: the proving in practical details of the lessons He teaches. This is just as much under His personal guidance and direction as the truth in theory is received directly from Him.

So He Himself provides for, and creates, the relationships of communion through cleansing, and intelligence through the indwelling of the Spirit, which constitute our condition for receiving what He has to teach.

What Can I Do?

Now, upon what personal conditions may I become a disciple? If I would have this enduement of pardon, cleansing, and illumination, how can it come about? No school of man was ever so strictly guarded, so select, as this. Yet none was ever so easy of access. No bar of race, or color, or caste, or age stands across the entrance. *Humanity* constitutes the only claim. And yet, because of the importance of the truths to be revealed, and of the necessity to concentrate every power of the being to the understanding and realization of these truths, Jesus stands at the entrance. He forbids any to enter, save upon certain conditions. Here is what He says:

> *If any one comes to me, and does not hate his own father and mother, his wife and children, his brothers, and sisters, yes, even his own life—he cannot be my disciple* (Luke 14:26).

> *Anyone who does not carry his cross and follow me cannot be my disciple* (Luke 14:27).

> *Any of you who does not give up everything he has cannot be my disciple* (Luke 14:33).

The new relationship must be superior, in the urgency of its reliance on the claim of any earthly relationship; it must be considered and answered before any claims of the self-life. The Teacher demands that we take up the cross and so follow on, even though the process takes us through pain. Even more, we must take the deep spiritual vow of poverty, renouncing all, even possessions, counting every word He shall speak, and every truth He shall reveal, through whatever methods, as our chief and only wealth. In short, we must not be held, either by being possessed by others, or our own possessions. There must be a clean severance from all entanglement, and an utter and uncompromising abandonment of ourselves to Him.

Unless this happens, we cannot be His disciples. If this be our attitude, then, to us He gives pardon, cleansing, light; and so, becoming by relationship His disciples, and entering His school, we are ready for, and enter upon, our course of instruction.

If these conditions seem too stringent, remember what depends upon them. Character and destiny depend upon this question of discipleship. Jesus the Teacher does not come to impart information, or to satisfy curiosity. It is because the truth sanctifies and makes free that He reveals it. Apart from the revelation He has to make, there is no possible way to realize God's great purposes for us. Compare Himself and His teaching with the most sacred and beautiful of earth's loves and possessions, and these are unworthy of a moment's thought. They must all be removed from between Him and ourselves, so that we may know and do His will. Such attitude does not rob us of the enjoyment of all these things, so far as in themselves they are right. Rather, it adds to our joy.

Self renders it impossible to know Christ, when other loves and interests intervene. This breeds dissatisfaction with all else and makes the disciple sad and weak. Christ, absolute, lights the whole being with His love, and joy, and beauty, and shines on other loves to their sanctification, and so, the abnegation of self is self's highest development.

So let us enter the school of Jesus, and, receiving His gifts, await His teaching.

2

Happiness is that after which all men in every age seek, and the first note in the Savior's teaching reveals it is what God is seeking also.

First Lessons

The Sermon on the Mount—as it is popularly styled, though the title always seems inadequate and poor—was delivered particularly to the disciples. The first and second verses of Matthew 5 very clearly declare this, "Now when he saw the crowds, he went up on a mountainside; and sat down. His disciples came to him; and he began to teach them, saying." The multitude followed and gathered around this little group of Teacher and taught, but the teaching was for the disciples only—that is, for such as were brought into that close relationship of which our first chapter spoke. Only those could follow who in some measure received the Teacher's wondrous words.

In actual experience the teaching of this sermon was too complex even for our advanced age. Men have hardly begun to guess at the glory and beauty of this wonderful ideal. But in relation to the Teacher it is elementary and initial. All the wealth of His wisdom—knowledge that He is waiting to impart—lies beyond anything said here. Here He deals with the first ideals of true life, and He reveals to men the divine purpose for them today. These are His first lessons.

Any complete and exhaustive exposition of all the wonderful and delicate detail here is impossible. It is not, indeed, the purpose of this study. A general analysis of the whole, that we may catch its sweep and scope, and obtain an outline of the system, is what is possible and necessary. We will now proceed to this consideration, noticing seven points of importance. I would suggest that you follow along the path of these points with your Bible at your side, tracing its teaching as you move through Matthew 5, 6 and 7.

Supremacy of Character (Matthew 5:1-12)

The very first word that falls from Jesus' lips is a revelation of the will of God for man: "Blessed." "Happy." That is the divine thought and intention for us. Sorrow, tears, pain, disappointment, all these may be, and are, of inestimable value in the Father's discipline; but they are means to an end, made necessary by man's sin. The end, in the purpose of God, is blessedness. Happiness is that after which all men in every age seek, and the first note in the Savior's teaching reveals it is what God is seeking also.

How, then, is it to be realized? This section contains the Master's answer. Men hold two views of what happiness consists, *i. e.*, having, and doing. To possess much, or to do some great thing, constitutes the sum of human blessedness according to popular theory. Our Teacher sweeps these conceptions away by absolutely ignoring them. No "blessed" of His lights up for man either the "having" or "doing" of man. *Being* is everything. A man's happiness depends upon what he is in himself. These "blesseds" of Jesus touch human life in its lowliest phases, and reveal the highest possibilities that lie before us. Henceforth, for the disciples of Jesus themselves, and as a basis for their estimate of others, *character* is to be supreme. On its positive side, there is infinite tenderness in this. On the negative side, it is stern and inexorable. Such teaching will produce lives running contrary to all worldly estimate and custom, and discipleship will mean persecution. Thus, the Teacher adds a "blessed" for those who suffer through character.

Influence the Intention (5:13-16)

This respect grows out of the former truth, and is at once the statement of a *fact* and the declaration of an *intention*. The fact is that character is apparent to others. If a man lives in the atmosphere of the beatitudes of Jesus, his life will exert certain influences. This is not only a fact, it is part of the divine intention. Savorless salt and light under a bushel are worse than useless; this is, however, the statement of an impossible hypothesis. Savorless salt ceases to be salt. Light under a bushel goes out. This the Master wants us to understand, and hence the terrific force of His figures of speech.

These symbols distinctly mark for us the influence that the blessed life exerts. Salt is antiseptic, pungent, preventing the spread of corruption. A wound that is healing will "smart" and sting when touched by salt. Absolute corruption, on the other hand, never smarts. When men smart under the influence of the antiseptic life of righteousness, it is a sign for which we should be thankful. When this happens, conscience is not altogether dead. We are not "past feeling." Disciples today, then, are to be salt, preventing corruption, and arousing the dormant sense of health.

Light is here used, I think, in the sense of guidance. Men are groping after God in this age with no light of their own by which to find Him. Your life as a disciple is to be a light, by the aid of which men come to glorify God. Let no man whose life fails to be antiseptic, and authentic, and never helps another Godward, imagine himself living within the circle of beatitudes.

The New Moral Code (5:17-48)

Having thus seen supremacy of character as the secret of happiness and the source of influence, we ask what are the laws which govern the development of such character. The new code of ethics is startling. When compared to this, the Mosaic law of conduct was easy to obey. The former is done away in the sense in which the less is included in the greater. Greater it surely is. Let this section be carefully read, remembering the following points:

The righteousness of the disciples is to exceed that of the Pharisees, as inner purity exceeds external whiteness.

Gifts on the altar do not atone for wrongdoing.

To look on sin with desire is sin; in other words, suppression of sin is still sin, because it recognizes the presence of a principle antagonistic to God and excuses it.

Retaliation is forbidden, and love is to be the one law of relationship. No one can reverently study this ideal of life without seeing the necessity for fulfilling the conditions of entrance to discipleship.

Self-abnegation (chapter 6)

This chapter may, and undoubtedly does, contain a great deal of teaching along other lines, but the underlying principle is that of self-abnegation. Note how the injunctions run counter to every popular idea of life:

- Alms are to be given privately, not blazoned abroad.
- Prayer is preeminently a matter between the soul and God. It is certainly not to be a means of advertising self-piety.
- Men are still to fast, but with glad face, not "appearing" so to do, so that self is to receive no glory for its denial of itself.
- Wealth is not to be held, save on trust.
- Self is to be so that anxiety concerning necessities cannot exist.

Surely never were self-consideration and self-consciousness so smitten hip and thigh as here.

Relative Charity (7:1-5)

The consideration of my brother's fault should drive me to self-examination rather than to pass judgment on him. I am ever to count my fault a "beam" in my eye and only a mote in his.

The Open Treasure House (7:7-14)

How tenderly and lovingly the Savior speaks in those verses. Just as one's spirit is in danger of being overwhelmed with the sense of the impossibility of realizing such ideals, He reveals to us the wealth that lies at our disposal in the love and power of the Father. In simple and easily understood words, He reveals our privilege in that matter. "Ask." "Seek." "Knock." For daily help remember the acrostic here. Take the initial letters A, S, K, and reflect that the words for which they stand reveal the secret combination that admits us into the treasure house of love. There is stored for us all that we need for the realization of the ideal.

Warning (7:15-28)

Now come solemn words of warning! Siren voices will seek to lure us. No teaching but His can produce true character. The truth of every message is to be tested by the life of the Teacher, and if failure is found there, we are to know him for "false" no matter how cleverly the sheep's clothing conceals the ravening wolf. How careful we need to be, lest we be led astray by specious teaching which is contrary to His will.

These lessons are all initial, lying at the very foundation of all Christ has to teach men. In proportion as they are realized He is able to lead us forward to deeper truths. An English Bishop said that this Sermon on the Mount could not be applied to the state. Whatever the Bishop intended, there is an aspect in which he was perfectly correct. These principles cannot be carried out in any state, save where the Kingship of Jesus is recognized, and men are His disciples. Only true disciples can understand, much less obey, His teaching.

The crowds leaving the mountain were impressed with the authority of the teaching, but they were not captivated with its beauty, for all this was beyond their comprehension. Christianity did not come by force of arms, nor could it. Christianity will never come by legislative acts. The wisest of earth's scholars, and the most astute of her politicians, can lift no finger to help the Kingdom of God save by coming in to the school of Jesus, learning of Him by the inshining of the Holy Spirit.

Look at that lonely, laboring soul in an isolated village, or far-off heathen hut, who is spelling out under the unique Teacher the lessons of this great deliverance. Such a one is building character on these sayings of Jesus and is doing more to realize on earth the Kingdom of God, than all the company of diplomats and politicians, who are forgetful in all practical things of the Nazarene. To the learning of these first great lessons now let us turn with all submission of spirit and surrender of life.

3

I must have daily personal communion with Him—study of His Word, waiting upon Him in prayer, the cultivation of close fellowship, telling Him everything—joys as well as sorrows—and periods of silence in which my soul simply waits and listens in the stillness for His voice. I cannot neglect these exercises without a film, a veil, a cloud of darkness coming between my soul and Himself, hindering the possibility of advancement.

No matter how dull the scholar whom He
    Takes into His school, and gives him to see;
A wonderful fashion of teaching He hath
    And wise to salvation He makes us through faith.
The wayfaring men, though fools, shall not stray,
    His method so plain, so easy His way.
                                    —*Charles Wesley*

THE METHOD
OF ADVANCEMENT

The subject of this chapter is not intended to suggest that all the "First Lessons" with which the last chapter dealt must be realized to the full, before spiritual progress can be made. The thought is rather that of gradual advancement in those first great lessons. They contain a statement of the full possibilities of character in these days of probation, and therefore it would be impossible to go beyond them in this respect. At the same time, it must be remembered that Jesus said much more than this to

His disciples, helping them to understand many of the things of God that had to do with their ultimate destiny and the divine purposes for the race. After all His teaching, at the last He had to leave them, saying, "I have much more to say to you, more than you can now bear. But, when he, the Spirit of truth, comes, he will guide you into all truth" (John 16:12, 13). Learning the First Lessons will create that character to which the deeper things of God become intelligible. Thus, advancement in the understanding and realization of these fits us for receiving and understanding whatever else may be beyond. The consideration of this chapter will answer the queston: "How, then, can we advance?"

Right Relationships with the Teacher Must Be Maintained

If we fail to understand this we fall into one of the subtlest dangers to which the disciple is exposed. Many believe that at some set time, through some special season of blessing, one enters into right relationships with Him. It is assumed that therefore, through all the coming days, these relationships abide. This is absolutely false. In all the realms of life there is nothing more delicate, more vulnerable than our relationship with the Master. The most tremendous forces man knows anything about can be set in motion by the simplest methods, and they may be hindered by means equally simple. So it is with this greatest of all forces—the cleansing and illuminating confrontation with Jesus. By simply ceasing my aimless activity I can come into living contact with my Lord—or by a moment's self-assertion, I may hinder His working. That is why I need to live daily and hourly and every moment at the very place of beginnings, ever as a child *depending* upon Him, and ever as one of the weakest of those who love Him, *abiding* in Him.

It is a glorious thing to know that my cleansing and illumination depend upon Him, that the whole of my responsibility in this matter is to maintain personal relationship with Him. The importance of this practice is, however, inexorable. I must have daily personal communion with Him—study of His Word, waiting upon Him in prayer, the cultivation of close fellowship, telling Him everything—joys as well as sorrows—and periods of silence in which my soul simply waits and listens in the stillness for His voice. I cannot neglect these exercises without a film, a veil, a cloud of darkness coming between my soul and Himself, hindering the possibility of advancement.

All this specially needs emphasizing in an age characterized by rush and unrest, loss of the old spirit of meditation and quiet. This characterization certainly applies to Christendom today, in our over-organization and never-ceasing rounds of meetings and activities. All this doing militates against moments of retirement and true worship. Personal relationship cannot be maintained in crowds. The Master and I alone is my perpetual need—and I must allow opportunity for that meaningful fellowship.

The Truth Taught Must Become Incarnate in the Disciples

As we emphasized at the outset, discipleship is not a condition for amassing information. Every doctrine has its issue in some clearly defined duty. Every theory taught reveals a practical application and responsibility. To the soul in right relationship with the Teacher, He reveals some new aspect of truth, and straightway there occurs some circumstance in which that doctrine may be tested by duty. We are most real in everyday circumstances—our true selves appearing then, rather than in the heroic and extraordinary days of life. The simple and commonplace experiences provide the testing places for our character. The circumstances that surround the disciples are in the hands of the Supreme Lord who teaches. He manipulates them and arranges for the advancement and development of His own. This is a great comfort. He knows the capacity and weakness and strength of everyone in His school. His examinations do not consist in a common testing for a common standard. Thus, they are not competitive. They are rather individual, special care being taken with each one. Peter will learn the supreme lesson of love with John, but the opportunity for manifesting it as a force in life will be separate and special in each case.

Advancement is dependent always on our obedience in these hours of testing. We practice in everyday life the power of the truth we have heard in theory. No lesson is considered learned in the school of Jesus, if it is merely committed to memory. That lesson only is learned which is incarnate in the life. It becomes beautiful in its realization and declaration in that way. Until this is so there can be no progress. Jesus said, "If any man chooses to do God's will, he will find out whether my teaching comes from God or whether I speak on my own" (John 7:17). The teaching of Jesus is cumulative and progressive. To attempt to learn the lessons of tomorrow without knowledge of today's would be utterly foolish. Just as no student can intelligently solve a problem in mathematics until he knows the definitions and accepts reasonably the axioms, so surely no disciple can possibly make progress in the truth of God, save as the first steps are taken. You cannot leave first principles and go on unto perfection, save as these first things have become practices, and not just theories. Life must go on a step at a time.

Here we touch the secret of much of the failure in Christian living today. Powerlessness in service, unattractiveness in life, what do they mean? Has the system of Jesus failed in these lives? Have the great lessons He came to teach humanity broken down in practice? Take any single example. It may be based on your own experience. When you first became a disciple, your days were days of delight and joy. The words and will of the Master thrilled and comforted you. You walked in His ways with a joy and gladness that filled the days with song. The people you touched in daily life saw the beauty of Jesus in you. Gentle and long-suffering, strong and pure, you incarnated His lessons. Your heart was glad, and other lives were influenced Godward.

All this has now changed. Prayer has become a duty. The Scriptures are dull and burdensome. You have no quick sense of the Lord's will. Your Christianity has become a prison, an encumbrance. These are confessions you never make, but they tell the true inner story of your life.

What does this really mean? Just this. One day in the past the Teacher gave you some new vision of truth that straightway revealed an opportunity for you to know the glory of that truth in the pathway of obedience. Something needed to be given up. Some action needed to be taken. Some word needed to be said. You paused, argued, disobeyed. Since that day no other lesson has been given, nor can it be. Every succeeding day depended upon your obedience. The experience was not final. It was preparatory, and until that is learned by obedience there can be no advancement, and so for weeks, perchance months, maybe even years, you have been a disciple making no progress. You have been stationary and static. No wonder you are weary of it all. The Teacher's love is marked in your case by His fidelity to Himself and His own lessons. Time after time, in meetings, in conversations, in loneliness, He brings you back to that point of beginning, and He reiterates with persistence and patience that passes all human understanding. "If any one chooses to do God's will, he will find out . . . ."

All progress in one's life was hindered for years because a letter was not written. Then I saw his face the day after that letter was mailed. The old light was restored, and the old joy returned as the great Teacher again began to reveal His will.

Advancement Can Only Be Within the Limit of Divine Purpose

God has an ultimate purpose, some place of high service farther on, and out of sight, for me. There is a glory and fruition beyond these days of learning and probation, a *being* and a *doing* for which all the teaching and discipline of today are preparing me. But it is also true that, as part of His great progressive movement, He has an *immediate* purpose in every life. We are workers together with Him *today*. There is no waste of time or material in the divine plan. Every step He takes us, every word He speaks to us, every testing He permits us, contributes something toward our development and progress.

Look at Joseph sold into slavery, or David exiled from his kingdom. See Job crouching under the whirlwind, and Paul bearing the buffeting of Satan's messenger. These experiences are examples. They were dark and mysterious at the time, and they formed part of the individual training of these men. But they were also in each case a necessary part of the divine dealing within the larger circle.

At the time, these men were principally conscious of limitation, and consequent longing for larger revelation. But before the experience was over they all came to understand that their suffering was for the sake of others. This was for them more than compensation for their restriction and waiting.

There are many things we do not know now because the greater issues would be hindered by our knowing. So what is best, the Teacher holds in reserve. He wants us, moment by moment, to bear our share in this march of God to ultimate triumph and light.

This section of our study is a most solemn one. Many disciples in name only have ceased to be taught of Jesus. We are all in perpetual danger of slipping out of the real circle of discipleship. For that reason we ought to ask ourselves the questions suggested by these three points on the subject of advancement. We should ask ourselves these questions regularly and always in the hour of loneliness with the Master.

First, am I in right relationship with the Teacher today? Do I still live at the Cross and know the power of its cleansing moment by moment? Am I walking in the light, without which all the words of Jesus are dark sayings, and His testings crosses, burdens out of which I can only gather reasons for murmuring?

Secondly, if I am not in this place of maintained fellowship, how did I stray? What word of His have I disobeyed? To that point let me return, whether it be but an hour ago, or years, and there let me absolutely surrender, at whatever cost. Let me do what He requires, however small, or however irksome it appears to be.

Third, am I content to wait when He seems to be silent?— and can I be patient as He accomplishes His present purpose in me, even though I do not understand it just now?

With matchless patience and pity, and tender love beyond all attempts at explanation, this Teacher waits, and stoops, and woos us. He is ever mindful of our highest good and deepest peace. Let us then, by consecrated watching, maintain the attitude of advancement, and so, line upon line, precept upon precept, here a little and there a little, as we are able to bear, He will lead us on, until we come to the perfect light and life and love of God.

4

No truer foreshadowing of heaven can
be found than the Christian home, with
all   its deep love, quiet peace, and
constant brightness.

Thus it is with the homely life around,
 There bidden, Christ abides;
Still by the single eye forever found
 That seeketh none besides.
When hewn and shaped till self no more is found,
 Self, ended at Thy Cross;
The precious freed from all the vile around,
 No gain, but blessed loss,
Then Christ alone remains—the former things
 Forever passed away;
And unto Him the heart in gladness sings
 All through the weary day.

—H. Suso

THE DISCIPLE AT HOME

So far we have considered the great essential facts of discipleship. There is a sense in which we hold most tenaciously that view of Christianity which is spoken of by some today as "otherworldly." Man's destiny lies beyond this life of probation, and toward that great issue the Master is ever working as He teaches us the lessons of His love. Yet it has ever been the glory of Christianity that it is intensely practical, touching the present life at every point with healing and beauty, sweetening all the streams by purifying the sources. In this and the following chapters it will be our purpose to trace the effect of discipleship on the common relationships of life.

We begin then with the disciple at home, because of its paramount importance. Perhaps there is no side of life more in danger of being neglected in this busy, many-sided age, than that of the home. And certainly there is no side which we can less afford to neglect. No service for God is of any value which is contradicted by the life at home. Neither have we any right to neglect our conduct at home because of our frantic "busyness" outside.

The home of the disciple may be conducive to progress in grace, or it may be quite the opposite.

The great ideal of the Christian home is clearly presented in the New Testament.

Facing the Facts

To the follower of Jesus Christ, there are certain central and unalterable facts which will touch and influence all the home relationships. Let us look first at these.

A new authority stands in the forefront. The Teacher has claimed an absolute and unvarying supremacy over the disciple's life. That initial condition of discipleship now enters into every question. There can be no deviation from it. This authority sets up the ideals of life, and declares the course of action in all the larger and more important matters of our days. It also governs the most simple and trifling details of my life.

The Teacher's authority becomes the gauge and measure of all other government. The rightness or otherwise of any rule of life imposed on the disciple by any other person is to be tested by the Will of the Master. So my obligation to any person as a disciple is limited or enforced by my supreme obligation to Jesus. Responsibility to Him is higher than that of wife to husband, or child to parents, or servant to master. These are all relationships of His approving, but His claim is first. If any of these relationships clash with my relationship to Him, they are to be set aside.

Then comes the new attitude created in me toward others. The relationship of the disciple to Christ, as we have seen, is that of life. In essence, Christianity *is* Christ. The disciple's life *is* the life of Christ. This life now becomes my governing force, and so it gives new character to my attitude and actions toward others. His Life is Love. That life, reigning in me, creates the disposition of love toward all. The old scheme of life glorified self. All other interests were made subservient to *my* needs, and all other persons were loved or disliked as they ministered to or interfered with "me." Now, as love governs our lives, each will "consider others better than yourself" (Philippians 2:3). The need of the "outsider" will become the touchstone of my life. The light of Christ's presence will reveal my own shortcomings, and the hitherto unrecognized excellencies of others. So the attitude of the disciple will become like that of his Lord—the attitude of one who waits not to be ministered unto, but to minister. The bearing of the cup of cold water to the thirsty will be the delight of all my days, opportunities I will not wait for, but will seek after.

Out of these essential considerations there grows a new sense of what home really is. It is to be the first, and perhaps the most simple and beautiful, manifestation of the authority of Jesus. Every member of the home, recognizing that supreme Kingship, will find his relationship toward other members of his family ennobled and purified by His love. Each member will be willing to deny personal aims for the sake of the highest good of all. No one will desire to gratify any part of his own desire at the expense of another. This self-abnegation, the sacrifice of my individual needs to the general peace and restfulness of others, will make home a heaven on earth. As the beatitudes of Jesus are allowed to rule my conduct at home, every sacred tie becomes in itself more delightful and satisfying. Christ's mission among His disciples is ever the *fulfilling*, and never the *destruction* of all high and noble ideals. The real music and beauty of home are only known to those who are simple and faithful disciples of Jesus.

Paul's Picture

What a glorious picture is presented of a true home in the writings of the apostle Paul. Although he himself was probably a widower and did not know the joy of such life, he nevertheless understood its beauty. If the student will take the different words Paul writes in his Epistles as to the true position and duty of husband, wife, parent, child, master, and servant, he will see the vision of the perfect home life. Let us look at the principal points.

Husband and Wife

Take first the husband and wife in their relation to each other, and as parents toward their children. What more wonderful ideal than this can there be? "Husbands, love your wives, just as Christ loved the church and gave himself up for her" (Ephesians 5:25). That is true love. It is absolute self-abnegation, the one overpowering passion being that of the highest good and greatest happiness of the wife. In such love, the thousand little neglects which can mar the life of a woman are impossible. How far more impossible the selfish brutality that too often has made homes infinitely more like hell than heaven.

Another command: "Wives, submit to your husbands as to the Lord" (Ephesians 5:22). That directive can only be obeyed when the husband is loving with the Lord's love. When that is so, see how beautifully there is recognized here the true view of woman's love. It finds its highest manifestation in submission.

Then the revelation of Paul's writings concerning the relation of parents to children is a remarkable one that sorely needs restating in these days. What is the father's responsibility? He is to *train* his children. Note how tenderly this is to be done: "Fathers, do not exasperate (provoke) your children; instead, bring them up in the *training* and instruction of the Lord" (Ephesians 6:4).

In this same passage, note the position of the child: "Children, obey your parents in the Lord . . ." (Ephesians 6:1). What a glorious and tender thought this is. It implies submission to an authority which frees the tender life from the responsibility of thinking and planning. It provides for an advance toward perfection, within the realm of a very definite and direct government. How grand a provision that is. Perhaps we never fully realize the blessing of childhood until we have passed beyond it. Amid the strife of life, with its oft-recurring crises, we are bewildered as to which path we ought to take. Then we long for the days of childhood again, when we could depend on father or mother. In obeying them we knew we were doing that which pleased the Lord. That view of obedience as the Lord's tender provision for our safety and development should ever be presented to our own dear disciple-children. How important it is that we parents seek parental wisdom from our divine Parent.

Then there is the presence in the home of those who help and serve. Their position is made very sacred in the school of Jesus. Most distinctly is it laid down that they can do "all things" as unto the Lord, and that expression includes and lights up the most trivial duties that they are called upon to render. It is of such that the wonderful possibility is declared, that they may "adorn the doctrine of God our Savior." How beautiful the life of some is, we know full well. Toward them the Christian master is to exercise the patience of his Master toward himself, making demands on eager, loving service, not by threatening, but by loving.

This is a glorious picture. No such ideal of home has ever been presented to the world. It has been realized in a large measure over and over again. No truer fore-shadowing of heaven can be found than the Christian home, with all its deep love, quiet peace, and constant brightness. Discipleship has often to be maintained in very different home surroundings. The husband, wife, parent, child, servant, may either of them be the only disciple, and their relationship to Christ looked upon with pity, contempt, or even open opposition. The position of such is very difficult; but for this, as for all other circumstances, the grace and power of Christ are sufficient. When this is so, there is a twofold responsibility resting upon the Christian:

First, remembering the great ideals, there must be *a realization of the Master's will for the individual*. The Christ-life of love must govern and manifest itself toward others, even though there be no return on the part of the dearest earthly friends.

Then, if that manifestation bring contempt and persecution, there is to be *an absence of the revengeful spirit*, and the presence of loving patience. By this, the unbelieving may be won by the behavior of the believing.

The creation of true Christian homes is the splendid possibility of young discipleship. The question of marriage lies at the base of this. Unequal yoking together of the disciples of Jesus with unbelievers is one of the most disastrous matters for the Church—and the world. And there should be no alliance of life even between believers unless the Lord's will be so clearly revealed that there can be no mistaking it.

The ideal Christian home will radiate outward to the world an atmosphere of love that will permeate and penetrate.

5

A Christian cannot enrich himself by
the downfall or failure of another. That
one who strikes a bargain to his own
profit at the expense of some
unfortunate does not belong to Christ.

Yea, we know that Thou rejoicest
O'er each work of Thine;
Thou didst our ears and hands and voices
For Thy praise design;
Craftsman's art and Music's measure
For Thy pleasure
All combine.

—*F. Pott*

THE DISCIPLE AT BUSINESS

There is no more common mistake, or one more dangerous, than to consider work as in some way connected with the curse. Man was created for work. It is one of the very first laws of his being. Unemployed man is a contravention of the Divine purpose. Before man fell, we see him in all the strength of his perfect being—at work. "The Lord God took the man and put him in the garden of Eden to work it and take care of it" (Genesis 2:15). Sin brought weariness and disappointment, and these

51

made work a burden. But work itself is a divine arrangement for the gladdening of life.

Of Fowls and Flowers

This law abides under the Christian dispensation. No word Christ spoke can be construed to revoke the value of work. It is rather taken up and enforced by Christ Himself and the apostles. In the "Sermon on the Mount" the Lord recognizes the power to work as a special gift which raises us above the level of birds and flowers. Of the fowls He said, "Are you not of much more value than they?" (Matthew 6:26). Of the flowers He said, "If this is how God clothes the grass of the field . . . will he not much more clothe you?" (6:30). In each case, the teaching is not that we should neither "sow" nor "reap," and neither "toil" nor "spin," but that, having these powers and using them, how much more likely it is that *our* need should be supplied—rather than that of mere fowls or flowers. The philosophy of the situation is that Christ recognizes all gifts and callings as from God. He looks upon them as the channels through which God will supply our need.

Paul is most clear in his exposition of the will of God in these matters. In 2 Thessalonians 2:10 he makes working the condition of eating, and in Ephesians 4:28 he places working in antithesis to stealing. There he reveals the larger social responsibility when he says that a man is to work not merely for his own support, but "that he may have something to share with those in need"; and in his first letter to Timothy (5:8) Paul declares that "If any one does not provide for his relatives, and especially for his immediate family, he has denied the faith and is worse than an unbeliever."

We recognize the great truth of the solidarity of humanity. Each person is part of the whole, that the whole is incomplete in the incompleteness of any. Thus it is evident that all the great and increasing needs of humanity for this life are provided for by God in the gifts He has bestowed, to every man severally as He will. His will is ever the well-being and happiness of the creature. Every ability to do something which will be for the support of the worker, and at the same time contribute to the legitimate needs of others, is a divine gift, a divine calling. Capacity for brain work, dexterity of fingers, are each and in every variety of application, divinely bestowed. To dig—whether with spade, or plow, or shaft and machinery—is a calling of God. To construct with wood, or stone, or iron, for permanence or locomotion, is a divine gift. To see a vision and paint it, to hear music and translate it, to catch glimpses of truth and embody them in written form, these and all the thousands of various gifts bestowed upon men are of God. On every individual some gift is bestowed. Even those who, in these days of humanity's sin and sorrow, are from their birth limited in their powers, have *some* gift, if only the ability to love in a childish way. Not only the preacher, but every person has a calling of God, and the duty of each man to God, to the community, to himself, is to discover that calling, and therein to abide (see 1 Corinthians 7:20-24).

This is the great divine ideal from which humanity has wandered, to its sorrow, shame, and undoing; and as discipleship means a return to divine ideals through the teaching and power of Jesus, we must now apply these principles to the disciple as he or she enters business.

What Is My Gift?

The first serious question, then, for the disciple is, "What is the gift bestowed upon me, the calling of God for me?" The answer to that question is to be found within, rather than outside oneself. A gift ever means fitness. To every man God intends to make watches, He has given the necessary sensitivity of touch and patience of spirit. To every woman He designs to teach, He has given the attractive force and lucid gift that fits her to hold and teach her children.

Discipleship means facility for discovering the gift of God. The trouble is that many have thought that when we begin to touch these things our Teacher is uninterested. So we have made the greatest blunders of our lives in choosing our occupation, rather than setting ourselves to discover the divine calling. To the young disciple who reads this and who has not yet decided on life's work, let me say in all simplicity and confidence, *seek to find your right place in life by telling your Lord your sense of need, and asking for His direction.*

In this matter an enormous responsibility rests upon parents, that they seek to discover the Lord's purpose for their boys and girls, and then train them for that position. This can only be done by patient watching for the manifestation of the God-bestowed powers of each life separately. This cannot happen when in tender years we send our children out of our homes to live and so transfer our responsibility to others than those by God appointed.

How Do I Develop It?

Once I have discovered my gift, I must, by persistent application, seek to develop it. The disciple of Jesus, recognizing his calling in life as of God, cannot possibly treat it carelessly or indifferently. Every power of the will must be brought to bear on the application of the mind to the mastery of the subject in hand.

A Christian carpenter will master the use of every tool, and lay himself out to embody in his work the very spirit of the Christ.

A Christian doctor will leave no department of the great science neglected, or will devote himself with perfect consecration to that department for which God has given him the gift of a specialist.

The great advantage of discipleship is to be found in the recognition of my calling as one that is divine. Then I am sure that He who bestowed the gift understands it, and all my personal application to its mastery will be in the spirit of dependent prayer. Christian mechanics, tradesmen, professional men, should be the finest in the world, and would be, if they lived in the power of their relationship to Christ.

How Am I to Work?

Fully equipped for qualified service, the disciple now faces the sterner work of the years. Under the present conditions of life this is mostly done as the servant of others. Again, referring to Paul's words in 1 Corinthians 7:22-24, we see how the disciple is to consider his higher relationship to God. He "is the Lord's freed man," and he "should remain in the situation God called him to."

How does that affect his attitude toward his work? It lights it up with the glory of the divine. Each aspect of work becomes a part of the divine contribution to the need of the community. If I work in an office, or sell groceries, or paint a picture, or play an instrument, or set a limb, or anything that is an exercise of the divine gift, I do it, not as a means of livelihood first, but as a part of God's plan. So I become, down to the smallest detail of everyday life, "a worker together with Him." If I hold that view of life's work, I will be part of the solution, not a contributor to the problem.

How does abiding with God in my calling affect my relationship to my employer? It makes me treat him as though he were in my place and I in his. Hear the Teacher's own words, "In everything, do to others what you would have them do to you, for this sums up the Law and the Prophets" (Matthew 7:12). To that nothing can be added.

Of Principles and Practice

Finally, the disciple in business on his own account lives and acts within certain very clearly defined principles. He ever remembers that he is a steward of his Master. He possesses nothing, but holds on trust all he has. He is responsible to Christ for what he gets, the way he uses it, and the measure of his getting or holding. No disciple of Jesus can amass a fortune simply for the sake of possession. He may be prosperous in his undertakings, but his prosperity must ever mean increased opportunity for divine service. No disciple can oppress the employee in his wages. That wage should be, not merely the measure of keeping his servant's body and soul together, it should include provision for the culture of all that his being demands. We bandy about the term, "living wage." That is not the measure for a Christian paymaster.

A Christian cannot enrich himself by the downfall or failure of another. That one who strikes a bargain to his own profit at the expense of some unfortunate person does not belong to Christ. No Christian can take part in the monopolies of the day, which have as the very basis of their operations the enrichment of the few to the detriment of the many. There is nothing perhaps more destructive in commercial life today than the great monopolies. America is cursed by them, and England is threatened. No disciple of Christ can touch them and abide in the teaching of Jesus. The twofold law of life, enunciated by our Teacher, will purify commerce throughout, and nothing short of that will ever do it. "Love the Lord your God with all your heart and with all your soul and with all your mind . . ." and "love your neighbor as yourself" (Matthew 22:37-40).

Will It Work Today?

These are said to be impossible ideals for business life today. We reply that the very essence and genius of discipleship is the realization of the impossible. It is just because the Church of Jesus Christ has stood in the presence of His teaching and said "Impossible" that she has become so weak and powerless in the affairs of this busy age. Let us have a few men and women again who, as the early disciples in Pentecostal days, believe in Jesus and in the eternal wisdom of all His teaching. Let them be prepared to suffer the loss of all things rather than disobey. Then the potency and possibility of His ideals will begin to dawn on the world again as it did in those days, breaking up dynasties, revolutionizing empires, and turning the world upside down.

Nowhere is such work more needed than in the business world. And nowhere can we make better investment for the Master's Kingdom today than by rigidly purifying that corner of our world which we touch.

Let every disciple find his gift *from* God, cultivate it *for* God, exercise it abiding *in* God, and he will not only secure his own highest success, but will contribute his quota to the preparatory work of this dispensation. Thus he prepares the way for the coming of the King and the establishment of His Kingdom on earth.

6

To destroy my physical power is to weaken my mental. That is, for today at least, to limit the opportunity for the culture of the spiritual. Any form of play, then, that injures my physical powers or dwarfs my mental vigor, or takes away my spiritual sense, is impossible for me as a disciple of Christ. That play, and only that, which recreates, and so fits for larger service, is legitimate.

In that new childhood of the Earth
Life of itself shall dance and play,
Fresh blood in Time's shrunk veins make mirth,
And labor meet delight halfway.
—*J. Russell Lowell*

First Baptist Church
PLYMOUTH 8 INDIANA
GOSHEN, INDIANA 46526

THE DISCIPLE AT PLAY

So far there has seemed to be no contradiction of terms in the subjects which have come under our consideration. Among all Christians there would be a consensus as to the propriety of considering *the disciple at home* and *the disciple at business*. I do not anticipate any conflict of opinion as to the subsequent division of this subject. I can, however, imagine that there may be a doubt in the minds of some as to the title of this chapter. And yet it is of such enormous importance that to omit it were not

61

only to render the study incomplete but it would also do a positive injustice to the follower of Christ who, upon this of all subjects, is feeling his or her need of direct and wholesome teaching.

The fact that large numbers of young people lose their spirituality at this point is due, not to the inconsistency of play, but rather to lack of clear teaching on the subject. Because of this they fail to understand the true position of the child of God in reference to play. Let us apply ourselves to a twofold consideration—first to the *fact* of play in the life of discipleship, and then to the *limits* which are delineated for those who are learning of Christ in this as in all matters.

The very first truth to be understood and kept in mind is the *purpose of Christ* in the present probationary stage of human life. I have already emphasized the fact that the Master is preparing us for an end, which is beyond the present life altogether. By that statement I stand. However, it must be remembered that, while in Christ I gain more blessings than my fathers lost, the very first business of the great scheme of redemption and instruction is the restoration of man to the divine ideal of human life here on earth. The man who most truly manifests the beauties of human life in all its aspects, most truly proves his progress toward and preparation for the glory that has not yet been revealed. A human being developed on one side of his nature, to the damage or detriment of another, is by so much thwarting a divine purpose and damaging a divine ideal. This we readily admit in some cases. For example, we consider the development of "flesh" to be injurious to the spirit. It is just as true of a man who loses his power for constructive work in his abandonment to play. It is equally true of a man who cannot play because his power to do so has become deadened by ceaseless toil.

The power to laugh, to cease work, and frolic in forgetfulness of conflict, to make merry, is a divine blessing bestowed on man. Its absence in any case is as certain a mark of the blighting effects of sin, as is the frothy life of the one who devotes himself to miscalled "pleasure." This one never contributes anything to the work of his generation.

This power of "play" is based upon the wisdom of God, and His knowledge of the needs of His creatures. To all this, scientific fact bears witness. Doctors know the enormous value of prescribing change, exercise, cessation of toil, and pure amusement to restore a person's spirit. The result is better work, harder effort and clearer thinking. This, in turn, results in life of a higher order. And what is true medical science but a discovery of the laws of God for the well-being of the creatures of His love?

Jesus did not come to contradict or set aside any great law of human life, and most certainly He did not design anything but the highest development for man. He has come to interfere here as everywhere else, and to restore play to its proper place in every life. Though He gave His followers no set of rules, He has given them, in His teaching, great principles. Following these lead to a life perfectly attuned to Him.

Learn to Play

Before turning to the consideration of these principles, let me state something clearly. We live in an age of ceaseless activity. Over and over again we discover that activity is more worldly than godly. Every person, whether Christian or not, is necessarily caught up and carried forward in this whirl and rush. It is an absolute necessity, and therefore a solemn duty, that the follower of Christ should learn how to play within proper limits. This will make the disciple stronger for the stress of the age, able to confront its rush, restlessness, and weakness, with a clearcut testimony. The peace, quietness, and tremendous force of the life possessed by, and matured in, God will be his or her portion.

Perhaps I may put this most forcefully by means of a personal illustration. I have no magic formula for the delivery of the messages of God on Sunday. These messages come after being solemnly sought, not only by prayer, but also by stern application to study and thought. But often the process is facilitated by a Saturday afternoon in company with some fellow-disciple on the golf course. With my bag of clubs, driving a golf ball over, and sometimes into, bunkers, teeing up and sometimes holing out, I can stride over the grass and through the heather and sand, singing with perfect sincerity:

> "I feel like singing all the time,
>   My tears are wiped away;
> For Jesus is a Friend of mine,
>   I'll serve Him every day."

"Play" is a part of my life!

The Complex Nature of Man

Now let us look at the limits of play for the disciple. These are found by natural sequence, in that condition of life in which I never for a moment forget that I am Christ's. My loyalty to Him is unquestioning and constant. How will this one great principle affect my play? In two ways: *first,* in the realm of my personal realization of His purpose for me. *Second,* in my relationship with Him for the accomplishment of His purpose in all those with whom I come in contact.

As we have seen, the purpose of Jesus is the perfecting of my being. It follows, therefore, most clearly that my play must ever be recreative in character, and never destructive. Further, the complexity of human life must be considered. Man is neither just body, soul, nor spirit; separately He is body, soul, and spirit. Between these different sides of his complex nature there is the closest and most subtle inter-relation. He cannot possibly do injury to either side without injuring himself as a whole. To destroy my physical power is to weaken my mental capacity. For today, at any rate, that is to limit the opportunity for the cultivation of the spiritual.

Any form of play, then, that injures my physical powers or dwarfs my mental vigor, or takes away my spiritual sense, is off limits for me as a disciple of Christ. That play, and only that, which recreates, and so fits for larger service, is legitimate.

Limiting Play

Then further, I cannot in the power of the Christ-life live only for myself. My recreation cannot in any way involve injury to my fellow-being—even though doing so may seem to be of direct benefit to me. Let me not be misunderstood. I do not say that because one man abuses golf by wasting his time on it, I am not to play. I do say that if I see that golf has such a fascination for a friend of mine as to make him liable to neglect his sterner work, I am to be "narrow" enough to refuse to play with him. He should play the game for the *re*-creation it gives him, as I do. The relative law is that I only have fellowship, even in play, with a fellow-being upon the principles which are highest and best for him. I am never to lower myself to a standard below my own simply for fellowship.

Neither can I consent to be amused in any form by that which is debasing the life of those who amuse me. I have purposely avoided naming any forms of play save those that would be looked upon as legitimate in proper time and place by almost every Christian. I very strongly desire in this, as in every detail of life, to throw the disciple upon the Master for direct guidance. I say this because I am persuaded there is no other safe course. There is no other unfailing and infallible authority.

Jesus makes a specialty of every individuality, and He alone can do this. That which may be perfectly lawful and right for me may be seen as sin by my brother. On the other hand, that which I dare not do at the risk of losing my spiritual force, he may find conducive to his highest advancement.

Let each of us seek the Lord's direct pleasure, and be true to that, and there can be no mistake. By following human examples, however, or making others the standard of what one may or may not do, I will be constantly liable to get into places of positive danger.

These principles in application will be found most drastic, and yet will bring us into the air of perfect liberty. There are some forms of worldly amusement which are debasing and injurious. These are indulged in at the cost of the degradation and ruin to others. Against all these the disciple, by word and life, should be in constant protest.

One of the surest ways to combat such activities is to manifest in our lives the joyousness of discipleship. Our power to play purely and perfectly should be exercised as surely in the light of the divine love as when we pray or preach.

7

Oh, the comfort, the inexpressible comfort of feeling safe with a person, having neither to weigh thoughts nor measure words, but pour them all right out just as they are . . . .

If I knew you and you knew me—
If both of us could clearly see,
And with an inner sight divine
The meaning of your heart and mine,
I'm sure that we would differ less
And clasp our hands in friendliness;
Our thought would pleasantly agree
If I knew you and you knew me.

If I knew you and you knew me,
As each one knows his own self, we
Could look each other in the face
And see therein a truer grace,
Life has so many hidden woes,
So many thorns for every rose;
The "why" of things our hearts would
    see,
If I knew you, and you knew me.

—*Nixon Waterman*

THE DISCIPLE
AS A FRIEND

Of all the words in our language which have undergone change of meaning, perhaps none has been more abused than this word "friend." It has as its root meaning the thought of love, for it is really the present participle of the old Anglo-Saxon verb *freon*, "to love." In old time it spoke of the close union between two persons—other than relatives—in the bonds of sincere love for each other, love that made each one care for, and desire to serve, the other more than himself. It is too often used loosely. A man is my friend today if he is but a passing acquaintance, or if we are on speaking terms.

I want to write of the disciple as a friend in the older sense of comradeship—close heart-companionship. The word is a Bible word and comes from both the Hebrew and the Greek. The Hebrew word translated "friend" signifies an associate, and comes from the root "to pasture." So a friend is one of the flock, feeding together, sharing the very sustenance of life. The Greek word is the word "lover," and so is in perfect harmony with the thought of the English word used for its translation.

By virtue of his humanity, all the world over, man seeks for friendship. The life of the hermit, the recluse, is abnormal. It is contrary to the very genius of human nature for man to live alone. This desire for friendship grows out of the deepest necessity of his nature, he being created for others as well as for himself. Sympathy, love, service, are the very essentials of human nature at its best, and these demand an object. So, in the largest and most general sense, man is not intended to be alone.

In a closer consideration of this great law, we find among people this further necessity for personal friendship. Every person could not be a close companion of every other. The selective law of affinity draws two people together in an undefinable brotherhood, sometimes closer than the brotherhood of blood. We say undefinable, because it is often difficult to know why two particular persons are such friends. Affinity may mean conformity, agreement, resemblance; it is also the union of bodies of a dissimilar nature in one harmonious whole.

This law of personal friendship has held for all time. David and Jonathan have had their forerunners and successors throughout the generations of humankind. Now, in this, as in all other matters, Christ comes to fulfill and not to destroy. He sent His disciples out two by two. In this, I believe, He recognized this great necessity in human life. To this day in all Christian service and Christian living, the strength and joy of a strong personal friendship are almost beyond computation.

The Highest Form of Friendship

Facing the disciple in this matter of friendship is a great limitation. He cannot enter into any close bond, save with those who are, like himself, submitted to Jesus Christ. This is the highest law of all to him, and nothing that can possibly interfere with his relation to his Lord must be tolerated for a moment. The claim itself looks difficult and arbitrary, at first blush. But the infinite wisdom and love thereof has been evidenced by what happens in the lives of those who have disregarded it. Some have formed friendships with the world which have proved to be enmity against God. The reason is perfectly clear to those who have a true conception of what discipleship really is, and how radically it differs from all other life.

Remembering this, consider how discipleship is in itself a perfect qualification for the highest form of friendship. Disciples of Jesus are drawn toward each other by the natural law of affinity. His work in them fits them for a friendship of the strongest and most lasting kind.

First, there is the self-denial which He has enjoined upon them as the path to discipleship, and the condition of its continuity. If self be denied, the one most prolific source of dissension in the breaking up of friendship has been removed. With what strength we can love and serve if we have forsaken self, with all its unceasing demands.

Then there is the common consecration of the life to the kingship of Jesus. Two people, loving each other, and each able to say, "The life I live in the body, I live by faith in the Son of God . . ." (Galatians 2:20), have the will and the impulse of the One uniting them. That One, in way and work, is ever *love*.

Third, there is a commonality of interest. It is written of the hosts that gathered at Hebron, that they were of "one mind to make David king" (1 Chronicles 12:38). That common cause made a people, a nation, solid and strong. The same is true of friendship in Jesus. The disciple has nothing to live for but by word, and deed, and prayer to bring on the day of his Lord's crowning. When two such followers are brought into comradeship by natural law, and their friendship becomes hot with the common cause of a great purpose such as this, how strong and lasting must such friendship be.

The Nature of True Friendship

Remembering the limitation and qualifications of friendship let us now proceed to consider the friendship of disciples in itself. Each will cherish for the other a very high ideal of life, character, and service, no less than the will of God in each. The prayer of Epaphras for the Colossian Christians "that you may stand firm in all the will of God" (Colossians 4:12) is a delightful statement of the desire that disciple-comrades ever cherish for one another. Their friendship is ever looked upon as a means to that end. So the very heart of the golden rule is reached in such friendship, for each does for the other what he would have the other do to him. When this is so, there comes that delightful sense of rest and relaxation in each other's company which is the very essence of friendship.

Some years ago a friend gave me a quotation which I copied into my journal. It was from Mrs. Craik's *Life for a Life*, and I share it here as a beautiful expression of what I am talking about. "Oh, the comfort, the inexpressible comfort of feeling safe with a person, having neither to weigh thoughts nor measure words, but pour them all right out just as they are, chaff and grain together, knowing that a faithful hand will take and sift them, keep what is worth keeping, and then with the breath of kindness blow the rest away."

That is the abiding condition of; friends of Jesus. All necessity for reserve and hiding is gone, in the absolute confidence born of the certainty of high and unselfish love. This vulnerability to one another produces the true vision of each to each. I shall thus be able to recognize quickly all the excellencies in the character of my friend which perchance other persons may be slow to discover. He will see with clearest vision the points of my shortcoming and failure. Love is never blind, and we shall know each other more deeply and truly in that life of mutual love, than it is possible for one person to know another by careful calculation or closest critical observation. It has been said that "Love will stand at the door and knock long after self-conscious dignity has fallen asleep." This is only another way of expressing Paul's great word, "Love is patient, love is kind" (1 Corinthians 13:4). Because this is true, the clear vision of friendship ever demands our eager, consecrated service. Good as it is recognized will be developed by fellowship. Where that good is costing my friend much sacrifice and suffering, I can provide encouragement and fidelity. The shortcoming will be a matter concerning which my friend will mourn and pray in secret. He will speak to me in such tones of tender love that I will be won to the higher surrender which ever means victory and advancement. So together, and by the reciprocity of this holy comradeship, there will be a building up of each other, and a mutual growth in grace.

There is no higher or more wonderful description of the possibilities of true friendship in Jesus than that contained in Paul's words in Romans 12:15: "Rejoice with those who rejoice; mourn with those who mourn." That is true sympathy, and perfect sympathy. It is a perfect description of true friendship. The word sympathy has too long been robbed of its glory by the narrowing interpretation which has considered it only as the power "to mourn with those who mourn." That is the smaller and easier part of true sympathy. Sympathy is the power that projects life outside the circle of personality and shares the life of another, feeling the thrill of the other's joy, and the pain of the other's woe.

That can only be realized when the friendship is centered in Jesus. Is my friend in trouble, in difficulty, in temptation? I am his companion still, and the sorrow, the perplexity, the anguish are mine also. Can I leave him now he has fallen? Impossible. When he fell, I fell, and I shall not stand erect again until he has made even that fall a "stepping-stone to higher things." Is my friend in joy, in prosperity, in victory? I am yet with him, and the rapture, the success, the triumph are mine because they are his. Can I be jealous of his promotion? Again impossible. If he rises so do I, and all his advancement is my greatest progress, for we are one.

Blessed is the man who has such a friend. It is impossible to have many. I do not believe that it is the divine ideal that we should expect such. It is questionable whether any person, apart from the higher realm of relationship, ever has more than one such friend. Such a friend cannot be separated. Oceans and continents may divide geographically, but mutual love laughs at these. In daily service, prayer, and meditation, each is still with the other, and thinks, and plans, and works under the old influences. This friendship knows nothing of conventionality's little axioms, but abides in the great realm of love. Its actions may be strange to the outside beholder. Such friendship cannot be broken. Death is but a pause, wherein the one hears from the great silence the old voice, and feels drawing him thither, the old love. And the other waits in the splendors of that silence, with the Lord, for the coming of the friend whose song will add to heaven's music. Friendship is always beautiful, but the friendship of disciples, based upon the law of affinity, and conditioned and consummated in Christ, is without peer and beyond comparison.

8

The disciple at work for the Master is
really the Master working through the
disciple.

We are not here to play, to dream, to drift,
We have hard work to do, and loads to lift.
Shun not the struggle; face it. 'Tis God's gift.

Say not the days are evil—who's to blame?
And fold the hands and acquiesce—O shame!
Stand up, speak out, and bravely, in God's name.

It matters not how deep entrenched the wrong,
How hard the battle goes, the day how long,
Faint not, fight on! Tomorrow comes the song.
—*Maltbie D. Babcock*

THE DISCIPLE AT WORK FOR THE MASTER

Ours is preeminently the "busy" age. It seems everyone must be *doing* something. Nothing more clearly reveals the spirit of the age than the contrast between people's attitude toward work now, and perhaps fifty years ago. Then, it seems, the busiest endeavored to make it appear they did nothing. Today the laziest are most eager for their friends to think of them as overworked. There never was such a day of organizations, and meetings, and societies. The Bible, and particularly the apostle Paul, has something to say on the subject:

> *Not slothful in business; fervent in spirit; serving the Lord* (Romans 12:11 KJV).

> *He who has been stealing must steal no longer, but must work, doing something useful with his own hands, that he may have something to share with those in need* (Ephesians 4:28).

> *Make it your ambition to lead a quiet life, to mind your own business and to work with your hands, just as we told you, so that your daily life may win the respect of outsiders and so that you will not be dependent on anybody* (1 Thessalonians 4:11, 12).

> *For even when we were with you, we gave you this rule: If any man will not work, he shall not eat. We hear that some among you are idle. They are not busy; they are busybodies. Such people we command and urge in the Lord Jesus Christ, to settle down and earn the bread they eat* (2 Thessalonians 3:10-12).

> *If any one does not provide for his relatives and especially his own family; he has denied the faith and is worse than an unbeliever* (1 Timothy 5:8).

Yet this very multiplication of work has in it an element of danger, and one of the perilous sides to it has been the setting of unsanctified and even unconverted persons to work. Side by side with this demand for workers has come a rebound from that view of a "vocation" which culminated in priestism, and the fitness of a caste only for holy service.

As is so often the case, the rebound has gone beyond proper limits. We have rightly contended for the rights of all believers to familiarity with the things of God, and freedom to serve. We have wrongly extended to those outside the circle of discipleship the opportunity to help in the work of the Master. This has been to their detriment, giving them a false sense of security, and it has also caused serious injury to the work itself.

We must return to first principles. Personal relation to Christ is the only qualification for service. Apart from that, there can be none. On that occasion, when the crowds, having come by sea to Capernaum "seeking Jesus" asked Him, "What must we do to do the works God requires?" He replied, "The work of God is this: to believe in the one he has sent" (John 6:24-29).

Of that saying Dr. Westcott writes, "This simple formula contains the complete solution of the relation of faith and works. Faith is the life of works; works are the necessity of faith." It cannot be too strongly insisted upon, or too frequently urged, that they, and they only, who are disciples of Jesus, are called to—and fitted for—fellowship with Him in the great work to which He is pledged. If I am a disciple, I am therefore a worker, for the new life which creates my personal discipleship is the very life of Christ—compassionate, mighty, victorious. If I am not a disciple, I cannot do the work of God, for I am devoid of that life which alone is the divine compassion for man, and the divine energy for accomplishing the purposes of God.

So much we must agree upon: the disciple at work for the Master is really the Master working through the disciple. The result is oneness. That granted we may now proceed to consider the aim, the methods, the strength, and the results of the disciple's work. This we accomplish by a contemplation of the Master's work.

The Aim

Christ makes a great statement in John 9:4, ". . . we must do the work of him who sent me." This "we " of the revised version reveals that Christ identifies us with Himself in the great task of His work. We will best understand the force of these words by gaining a clear understanding of their context. Look back at chapter 8. In verses 1 to 11 we have the account of Christ's dealing with the woman taken in adultery. Then in chapter 9:6 and following we see Him giving sight to the blind man. Now, examine the part that lies between. His opening statement (8:12) and the closing (9:5) are identical: "I am the light of the world."

Growing out of that statement in chapter 8, we have a long controversy on inherited privileges and divine Sonship. In chapter 9, the disciple's question is in the same realm, though it deals with the other side, that of inherited sin.

Christ dismisses their speculations, and announces the fact of His work, and proceeds to illustrate it by another example. This at once answers their quibbling and reveals the true nature of that work. The blind man in chapter 9 is, as every man is, a revelation of the human condition, and an opportunity for the display of the work of God. What, then, is the work of God? The remedying of the limitation and evil that is in the world, and the restoration of the natural—that is, the divine purpose.

The illustration is simple. The underlying revelation is sublime. The divine rest spoken of in Genesis 2:1, 2 was broken by man's sin. From that point God has been at work. "My Father is always at his work to this very day, and I, too, am working" (John 5:17). This is not a small thing. It encompasses all in its scope. It cost all in its effort. The cross is the supreme expression of that divine work. This can only be understood when it is seen as the eternal force by which man's ruin and limitation are overtaken. In this the first divine ideal for humanity can be realized.

In the disciples of Jesus there moves that great life that works with ceaseless and unconquerable energy. "*Thy* will be done, *Thy* kingdom come," is the disciple's prayer; it is also the aim of all his life and work. In the home, the business, the political and national life, and the Church, we are "workers together with him," opening blind eyes, loosing prisoners, healing humanity's wounds, toiling ever on toward the morning without clouds, in which God will rest in the accomplishment of His purposes.

Our Methods

If our aim is identical with that of the Master, it necessarily follows that our methods must be identical also. By reading carefully (and in conjunction) John 5:17-19 and 14:10, we find that all His works and words were done and spoken, not on His own initiative, but only the will of the Father. That is to say, Jesus not only worked toward the same great consummation as His Father, but He followed along the same lines, and used the same methods. How very wonderful are these words, "The Son can do nothing by Himself, he can only do what he sees his Father doing" (John 5:19).

He goes on to say, "The words that I say to you are not just my own" (John 14:10). From this position the enemy directly and indirectly sought constantly to allure Him, and, thanks be to God, uniformly and absolutely failed.

In the wilderness He declined the kingdoms of this world, even though for these He had come. He did not choose on any condition, or by any method, to save the divinely marked. It is just here where the evil of the "mixed multitudes" in our churches is manifest.

The true disciple must be as particular about the methods of work as about the final issue; but so many have caught some faint idea of the divine intention, and now are prepared to adopt any method that seems politic and likely to achieve the end. And so the things that are worldly, sensual, devilish, are being pressed into the service of the churches—choirs of professionals, who give *performances* for their own glory, and *entertainments* which approach as nearly as possible to the world. The devil's most prolific move is the secularizing of the things of God, tempting men to seek to possess the kingdoms of Christ by falling down and worshiping him. The disciple-worker will not expect to find any "short cuts" to success, any more than his Master did, but he will travel ever by the way of the cross of offense and the resurrection of power. There are three main methods for the disciple, as it seems to me.

1. The *example* of the life, in all its details loyal to the Master;

2. The *influence* exerted by the character that is perpetually

growing in grace, by unbroken attention to the lessons of the Teacher, and the resultant incarnation of those lessons;

3. The specific *urging* of the claims of Christ upon others, so that no day passes in which an effort is not made to win a soul for Christ, by word spoken, or written, or intercession with God.

Our Strength

The next point is a remarkable one, and we approach it reverently, yet without hesitation. The strength in which the Master accomplished *His* work is that by which we are to accomplish ours! It is worthy of special note that Luke, whose second treatise (the book of Acts) is that which gives us the account of the coming of the Holy Ghost, and of His acts through the first disciples, very clearly marks for us our Lord's dependence upon that same Spirit. In Luke 4:1, we see Him returning from Jordan "full of the Holy Spirit," and "led by the Spirit in the desert." From that wilderness experience He enters upon the work of His public ministry, and in Luke 4:14, we are told He did so "In the power of the Spirit"; and in the passage He read in the synagogue at Nazareth, He claims the anointing of the Spirit for service (Luke 4:18). So, full of the Spirit, He lived, and was led of the Spirit. In that Spirit He went fearlessly through all the great conflicts of human nature, and "anointed of the Spirit" He undertook all specific service.

Before leaving His disciples, in those wonderful discourses John has recorded, He promised them that His Spirit should come "to be with them forever" (John 14:16), and that His mission should be to reveal to them the person and teaching of the Master (John 16:13,14).

Thus, then, the disciple goes forth to his work in the self-same strength as that in which the Master Himself went forth to His. The only understanding I can ever have of the purpose of God comes by revelation from the Holy Spirit, and the only force by which I can accomplish anything is by that of the self-same Spirit. What a glorious reserve of power there is in the Spirit-filled life, and the Spirit-anointed worker! All life becomes part of the great divine activity. Daily duties can no longer be drudgery, for every commonplace contribution to the day's necessities is done, for the hour present, and for the ages to come, toward that great consummation for which God works. Special forms of service have new meaning and new delight; for no word inspired of the Spirit returns void, and no work energized by Him is lost or worthless.

The Results

Of the results of our work, few words need be said. Again there is identity with Christ. "If we endure, we will also reign with him" (2 Timothy 2:12). If Christ ultimately fails, then the piece of work you did yesterday and are doing today will perish. If He accomplishes all His great purpose, then nothing I have done toward His end, by His methods, in His strength, can be lost. There will be a gracious and searching day of testing, when Love will burn up the hay, the wood, the stubble, and purify, to the brightness of the very home of God, the gold and silver and precious stones.

Let us, then, do better work by living nearer to the King, and know more fully the privilege and joy of service by a complete abandonment to Him.

9

Does God take pleasure in human suffering? Most assuredly not! He who created without sorrow will also wipe all tears away.

Yet sweeter even now to see Thy Face,
    To find Thee now my rest
My sorrow comforted in Thine embrace
    And soothed upon Thy breast.

Lord, there to weep is better than the joy
    Of all the sons of men;
For there I know the love without alloy
    I cannot lose again.

—H. Suso

The Disciple in Sorrow

Sorrow is the common heritage of humanity. In all ages, in all lands, under all conditions, man feels pain, and suffers anguish. Is sorrow, then, a part of the original divine intention for man? Does God take pleasure in human suffering? Most assuredly not! He who created without sorrow will also wipe all tears away. And yet today sorrow is a divine provision having an infinite meaning and exerting a marvelous influence. What Cowper sang is certainly true:

> "The path of sorrow, and that path alone,
> Leads to the land where sorrow is unknown;
> No traveler ever reached that blest abode,
> Who found not thorns and briars on his road."

Though sorrow came in the track of sin, it was not the companion and ally of it. No, it can be God's quick messenger, a sense of loss, opening at once the door back to the heart and home of His love. Sorrow is a deep sense of loss, the consciousness of lack, the natural experience of a God-forsaken life.

Had there been no dethronement of the King, there could have been no sorrow, for the whole being, still and quiet in Him, could have had no sense of loss. When man committed the act of high treason, by listening to a voice that called in question the love and wisdom of the divine authority, there sprang up in that moment the first sense of lust, *ennui,* hunger, and sorrow, and it took the form of a desire to know what God had not revealed. And when, following that desire, instead of returning then and there to allegiance man passed through the door, seeking liberty, he found himself in a darkening void. Without God. Yet he possessed a nature that made demands perpetually which neither he himself nor any other could satisfy.

The Man of Sorrow

Sorrow, then, is the result of sin, but it is the benevolent, tender, purposeful messenger of the eternal love. Our Father God cannot see His offspring lose all, without causing within them this sense of loss, and so ever by that means attracting them homeward. Carry out that view of sorrow, and see how wondrously the person and work of Jesus agree with it. The prophet, Isaiah, long before He came, spoke thus of Him: ". . . a man of sorrows, and familiar with suffering," and further declared "Surely he took our infirmities and carried our sorrows" (Isaiah 53:3, 4).

Turning from that sacred forthtelling of the *purpose* of the

Messiah's coming to the historical account of His life and work, I find the very heart and center of it reached on Calvary's cross. There He cried from the darkness into which He had passed, seeking that which was lost, "My God, My God, why have you forsaken me?" (Matthew 27:46; Mark 15:34). That is the greatest sorrow of all. There in the person of Christ all humanity's sorrow and anguish and tears are centered. That is the expression of all agony. Beyond that there is no sorrow. And that is also the great cry of humanity's sin; God dethroned by man; man forsaken by God. Beyond that there is nothing.

So He bore our griefs and carried our sorrows in that awful hour when He was wounded for our transgressions and bruised for our iniquities. There all the world's sin is borne and its sorrow felt. After that—silence. Surely a stillness in heaven, on earth, in hell—and then, "It is finished" from His lips, and He, the conqueror, died by "laying down" His life. Sin is put away, and sorrow is recalled. Righteousness commences her new reign and joy follows in her wake, the glorious possibilities of humanity are opened up, for Christ has lived and died, and lives forever now, and is a priest "on the basis of the power of an indestructible life" (Hebrews 7:16).

In that Cross there was the rediscovery of God to man, and the rending of the veil for man's return, and all healing provided. The appropriation of the purchased possession is, in the wisdom of God, secured by processes that cover centuries in man's measurement, and so sin is still here, and sorrow must therefore remain also. What, then, is the disciple's relation to it?

Rejoicing in Sorrow?

To the disciple the realm of sorrow has become circumscribed, in large measure. The great sorrows of humanity are personal and self-centered: some loss experienced, some injury inflicted, some disappointment realized. These are the common causes of sorrow. In proportion as self is subdued and God is enthroned in the life, this class of sorrows becomes obsolete. Increasingly, the soul finds its all in God. Thus it is able not merely to be resigned but to rejoice in denials as well as in blessings bestowed. Very slow we may be, even in the school of Jesus, but this is the growing experience of those who are learning of Him and are submissive to His teaching. This witnesses to the fact that God fills all the gaps, and brings the heart into perfect rest, are not wanting, neither are they few. "The heart at leisure from itself" has so learned of Jesus as to rejoice in exactly the circumstances that in the old life caused the keenest sense of sorrow.

Growing Through Sorrow?

From this is seen the mission of sorrow. It is ever a disciplinary force, drawing the heart more and more toward God, as it creates a sense of the hollowness and uncertainty of all that has been held most dear. How wondrously this is apparent in the life of the believer. Take two persons—one whose will is rebellious and whose heart is unregenerate, the other a disciple of Jesus—and let them pass through identical experiences of bereavement, affliction, failure, and disappointment. In the unbeliever the spirit becomes embittered and callous and the character degenerates; in the believer gentleness, love, tenderness are the results, and the very face catches a new glory and beauty. The one defiantly faces sorrow, and looking upon God's messenger as an enemy attempts to destroy or banish it. This person sinks into hardness and hatred. The believer, on the other hand, is drawn to the heart of God, he finds the pain to be God's fire for the destruction of dross. Thus his spirit rises into that ineffable sweetness and love which is such a revelation of the power of the God of Love.

The Secret of Sorrow

What, then, is the secret of this positive effect of sorrow upon the life of the disciple? It is the companionship of Jesus. He who touched the inner heart of all the world's agony is ever present, understanding the very deep meaning of that pain, the absence of God. He knew every form of anguish as He endured the Cross. No greater pain could have been experienced.

In your darkest anguish, O believing heart, what healed you? Was it not that Christ said to you, "I am just what you have lost, and infinitely more"? And as you said, "Yes, my Lord, You are," did not all the horizon kindle with a new light? All your pain is quietly eased by the magic of His own touch.

Divine Mathematics

Looking back over our sorrows since we entered the school of Jesus, there is yet another truth to be recognized. That is the fact of their certain change. When the Master was about to leave His earliest disciples, He said to them of the keenest pain of the time—the thought of His departure—"Your grief will turn to joy" (John 16:20). Didn't that change happen?

In the coming of the Paraclete they learned how expedient it was for them that He should go away. So in His going their greatest grief would become their greatest joy. In His Ascension and the consequent coming of the Holy Spirit into their lives, they entered a whole new dimension of spiritual life. This promise—"Your grief will turn to joy"—clarifies the whole philosophy of pain to a believing, trusting heart.

How perpetually sorrow can be turned into joy. This doesn't mean the sorrow is removed, and so joy comes. Rather, the sorrow itself *becomes* the joy. Have we not all had such experiences? Can we not look back and see that some of the hours that throbbed with agony were the most blessed of all the hours of life? That personal affliction, that blighting disappointment, that lonely hour of desolation, would you omit it from life's experience if you could? No, a thousand times, no. That affliction was the door to strength. The grave of that loved one was but the prelude to resurrection power. That disappointment resulted in the discovery of His appointment. That lonely hour was the one in which I found Jesus only. And so I come to understand that sorrow removes my ignorance and my limitation. By faith I learn to triumph even in the hour of darkness, having discovered that God's hand arranges warp and woof. He alone knows the perfect pattern. For that unfolding I wait and sing.

A New Realm of Sorrow

The disciple enters a new realm of sorrow. Union with Christ means a measure of "the fellowship of sharing his sufferings" (Philippians 3:10). "A heart at leisure from itself" is a heart able to "soothe and sympathize." Free from the blight of sorrow, I am able to see my sorrows as His choicest gifts. Leaving them ever with Him, I come to understand the awful needs of humanity. I go to His cross to be in some measure a sharer of His suffering for others. Out of that compassion comes all service that really does anything for humanity. There may be much activity in the self-life, but it is of little worth. As self dies on the cross, the new pain begins. So long as I remain here, the sorrow and sin of the world must press on my heart, for His life now holds and governs it.

And what is the end? Through all earth's pain and anguish what is coming? Let a seer of the old and new covenants each answer:

Isaiah: "The ransomed of the Lord will return. They will enter Zion with singing; everlasting joy will crown their heads. Gladness and joy, will overtake them, and sorrow and sighing will flee away" (Isaiah 35:10).

John: "He will wipe every tear from their eyes. There will be no more death or mourning or crying or pain, for the old order of things have passed away" (Revelation 21:4).

Hallelujah. Amen.

10

No man has power to perfectly enjoy
the present who cannot look the future
in the face with assurance.

My heart is resting, O my God,
   I will give thanks and sing;
My heart is at the secret source
   Of every precious thing.
                    —*Anna L. Waring*

THE DISCIPLE IN JOY

When Eliphaz the Temanite said, "Man is born to trouble as surely as the sparks fly upward" (Job 5:7) he expressed a fact of life. But he was not saying that this was in God's original plan for man. Under existing conditions man is so born, but trouble is contrary to God's original purpose. Rather, God desires the joy, the happiness, of all men.

Sorrow is an interpolation in the divine plan, necessary and beneficent as we saw in our last chapter. On the other hand, joy is the normal condition of man, God's highest work. Sad and sorrowful as the earth is today, man's capacity for joy is evidenced in the fact that, in the vast majority of lives, there are more days of happiness than sorrow.

In the face of overwhelming disaster in all areas of his being, man has set himself with indomitable courage to wrest happiness in some form out of his circumstances. Much of the so-called happiness of men is inexpressibly sad, and poor, and sinful. Yet the fact remains that the great bulk of humanity has set itself to seek for happiness. In that fact lies the evidence that God's original plan for man was joy. Every form of enjoyment that man has devised for himself is his attempt to reconstruct out of hopeless wreckage and ruin the glorious past. It is a heartbreaking picture, yet it is a lurid and appalling testimony to the magnificent possibilities of his being.

Following our earlier argument that sorrow is a sense of loss, we say that joy is the true condition of God's desire for humanity. As sorrow entered with the *loss* of the sense of God, so joy is restored as man *finds* God again.

Joy Restored

When the disciple is restored to communion with God, he is welcomed back to the place of joy. In writing to Timothy the apostle uses a remarkable word: ". . . whatever . . . conforms to the glorious gospel of the *blessed* God" (1 Timothy 1:11). The phrase might be correctly translated, "The *happy* God." It illustrates for us a great fact in the character of God. He is *blessed* for evermore, *happy* in the very essential core of His nature. Creation complete, He saw it as "very good"; and the "rest" of God was not recuperation after toil, but complacency, satisfaction, happiness in His work. The inspired seers of the past saw Him, and, though the surroundings of His throne seemed to them, to be clouds and darkness, their conception of Him was ever that of glory, beauty, strength, love, peace, happiness, and joy. When man fell, that very happiness of God inspired the movement toward man's recovery. Read the closing words of Zephaniah's prophecy (3:14-20), especially noting the seventeenth verse: "He will take great delight in you . . . he will *rejoice* over you with singing" (3:17). What words can more beautifully express His blessedness than these?

When Jesus, the express image of the Father, came, He gave us in many graphic pictures the same conception: the glad Father, the rejoicing shepherd, the happy woman—all teach the same truth. In the great charter of the kingdom, the Sermon on the Mount, He pronounces upon His disciples the same character. "Blessed" here may be as correctly rendered "Happy" (see Matthew 5). So those who are His today are restored to living communion with the "happy God." Thus they themselves are brought to the place where it becomes possible for them to obey the apostolic word: "Rejoice in the Lord always. I will say it again: Rejoice!" (Philippians 4:4).

All human joy is tarnished by the presence of the elements of fear and dread. Man cannot escape from the deepest facts of his own nature, and therefore in the midst of every form of pleasure there comes the unnameable, disturbing element of fear and apprehension. This may be concisely stated by saying: no man has power to perfectly enjoy the present who cannot look the future in the face with assurance. So long as the known specter of death haunts the consciousness of man with a vague terror, every gladness may be blighted in a moment. I do not speak of low forms of enjoyment, but of the highest types: Love, friendship, home, nature, art, music. All these suggest to the unforgiven soul the awful possibility of cessation, and then the unknown tomorrow becomes the tarnish on all gold.

The disciple in union with Christ has found the solution to all this mystery. He is at peace with the end, and so is free to bask in the true enjoyment of the "now." Because "to live is Christ," "to die is gain," and because "to die is gain" life is worth living, for the specter has been transformed into a gentle angel. This blessed being stands ever at the portal of a larger and more generous life.

Of Love and Joy

Now, how does this factor affect the life of the disciple? This twofold fact—communion with the blessed God and the consequent casting out of fear from the life—introduces into all pure human joy the element which perfects the same. The greatest of earth's joy lies in earth's love. The ties of home and family, the communion of friend and lover, how immeasurably are these joys intensified to the believer.

The union of two in marriage, based upon the law of supreme affection between them—when they are united in Christ to God—how holy, and restful, and satisfying to the heart! The presence in the house of children, when they are recognized as gifts of the eternal love, to be nurtured for the King—how glorious and blessed this relationship. The growth, development, and success of these when the King's laws are obeyed, what pure and full joy they bring.

Look at the other great avenues of enjoyment: nature in her thousand varying moods, art in its wondrous possibilities, music in its interpretation of pure thought and high enthusiasm. How the disciple enters into all these because in his relationship to Christ he holds the mystic key which admits him to their inner secrets.

Surely everywhere and at all times the anointed soul can see and hear, and touch, with keenness and precision that which is unknown apart from Christ. Never allow the enemy to suggest to you that discipleship is the limitation of joy. It is the one condition of human life today that opens every door of human delight and permits man to walk in the splendid spaces, perfectly at home in the happiness of the "happy God."

The greatness of this joy overtakes and overwhelms all the sorrows that remain to us.

"How many children have you?" asked one of a Christian father. Hear his reply, "Seven—five live with me, and two with Jesus." Surely this was rejoicing in sorrow. Did the father not miss the prattle of the tongues now silent, and the patter of the little feet in his home? Assuredly, he did. But he heard them still by faith in the palace home of God. And the joy of possessing some treasure of his very own there, was more than compensation. The joy of sorrow lies, moreover, in the fact that it introduces and prepares the disciple for the joy beyond. Of our beloved Lord it was said: "Who for the joy set before him endured the cross, scorning the shame" (Hebrews 12:2) and that marks our glad pathway through all the disciplinary sorrow of probationary days. To us, on every sorrow, falls the light of the joy beyond, and that not merely as compensation, but as result. So, while we are sometimes "sorrowful" we are "yet always rejoicing."

A New Joy

In our last chapter we examined the new sorrow that comes to the disciple in communion with Christ—sympathy with all the sin and sorrow of suffering humanity. Now, we must also recognize the new joy that springs out of service. To me it is difficult to speak or write of that joy. Have you ever led one soul to Christ? Then you know more than all words can teach you of the essence of real joy. To tell the good news, to pray with the seeker, to travail in birth for souls, to see the emergence of the light of God, to find another passing to His Kingdom, this is life and joy indeed.

Paul, the great missionary, the man who in those days of suffering and peril, so wondrously laid his whole being upon the altar of His Master's cross for other's blessing, could think of no greater joy in heaven than that of souls newborn through his toil and suffering. "For what is our hope, or joy, or the crown in which we will glory in the presence of our Lord Jesus when he comes? Is it not you? For you are our glory and our joy" (1 Thessalonians 2:19, 20). And surely that joy has its source in the divine joy. It is over a redeemed people that God "rejoices with singing," and it is in the accomplishment of the great purposes of the eternal Love that the Master "shall see of the travail of his soul, and be satisfied."

The great John Newton wrote:

> Joy is a fruit that will not grow
>   In nature's barren soil;
> All we can boast, till Christ we know,
>   Is vanity and toil.
> But where the Lord hath planted grace,
>   And made His glories known,
> These fruits of heavenly joy and peace
>   Are found, and these alone.

11

Disciples . . . are not called upon to prepare for death, but for *Him*. That hope purifies, refines, illumines all the hours with the radiance of the eternal day.

Soon the whole,
Like a parched scroll,
shall before my amazed sight uproll,
And, without a screen,
At one burst be seen
The Presence wherein I have ever been.
—*Thomas Whytehead*

THE DISCIPLE GOING HOME

When Bernard of Cluny wrote, "Brief life is here our portion" as the opening words of his great hymn, he penned a fact that is an abiding consciousness with people of all ages and every clime. The glory of the hope, and certainty of the faith which characterize that hymn, are beyond the experience of thousands, but that first statement finds an affirmative echo in every heart, whenever and wherever it is sung. This brief life is passing, and the number of our appointed years is becoming smaller. This

process follows a perfectly quiet and orderly path, yet it is irrevo-
cable and absolutely unalterable. The last year, the last break of
day, the last moment will come; and moreover, not a single one
among the millions of the race now moving on toward the end
can tell the year or day or hour of that end. These are solemn
and self-evident truths.

That end, called death, is at once the greatest certainty, and
the greatest mystery of all. To the consciousness of the natural
man there is no escape from it. Yet around it has gathered, for
the thinkers of all ages, and the teachers of all systems, and for
those also, who will not think, and who seek no teachers, a great
darkness and mystery. That is why man naturally shrinks from
death, and by every means in his power seeks to put off the day
which is his last. Yet, as people strive to do this they know how
futile is the strife. So, by some sort of common consent, unwrit-
ten and yet binding, people endeavor by a forced forgetfulness
to banish death and its awful dread. What then is the attitude of
the disciple toward this fact of the onward movement of this
present life toward an end?

An unknown poet has put it this way:

> Out of this life I shall never take
> Things of silver and gold I make.
> All that I cherish and hoard away,
> After I leave, on earth must stay.
>
> Though I call it mine and I boast its worth,
> I must give it up when I quit the earth.
> All that I gather and all that I keep
> I must leave behind when I fall asleep.
>
> And I wonder often, just what I shall own,
> In that other life when I pass alone,
> What shall He find and what shall He see,
> In the soul that answers the call for me?
>
> Shall the great Judge learn when my task is through
> That my soul had gathered some riches too?

Or shall at the last, it be mine to find,
That all I had worked for, I had left behind?

Let me try to answer his questions:

Facing the Fact

The answer may be very briefly stated first as a matter of fact. The disciple dares to contemplate openly that end. No longer shrinking from thought of it, he calmly faces it, questions it, smiles at it, and standing in its presence confronts it without fear or fainting. More than that, the disciple thus facing the end, from that very contemplation seems to catch a new radiance as of a light that never was seen on land or sea. His gaze into what the world has ever thought of as dark and mysterious gives his eye a joyous brightness. It tells of visions that add their luster and their hope to all the experiences of the passing hour. For the disciple, the contemplation of the end, instead of *shadowing* all the pleasures of the moment, fills the darkest day with light. It makes every hour of sorrow an occasion of rejoicing.

For the truth of this fact we can look to the experience of the Master Himself. The writers of the New Testament, and the followers of Jesus in each successive century, bear unequivocal testimony as well.

Let us confine ourselves to the experience of the Lord, and the testimony of New Testament writers. The writer of the letter to the Hebrews (12:2) gives us an inspired and remarkable vision of our Lord's view of the end of His human life. Here is the record: "Jesus . . . for the joy set before him endured the cross, scorning its shame, and sat down at the right hand of the throne of God." He saw the "cross" and "shame," and "endured" the one, "scorning" the other, for the "joy" that was set before Him. Of course this has a much wider application, but it certainly contains this revelation of our Master's view of the end of His life—the darkest and most mysterious end of all. What bulked most largely on His vision was a "joy" that lit the darkness, and negated the "shame."

The experience of the writers of the New Testament, as revealed in their writings, is on the same plane. Paul's writings abound with such conceptions. "I consider that our present sufferings . . . are not worthy to be compared with the glory that will be revealed . . ." (Romans 8:18). He tells the Philippians: "To die is gain" (Philippians 1:21). He writes to Timothy: "The time has come for my departure" (2 Timothy 4:6). These passages should, of course, be read in their entirety, and they are but examples of many others, all revealing the same truth.

Peter, looking forward, speaks of "a living hope . . . an inheritance that can never perish, spoil or fade . . ." (1 Peter 1:3, 4). James lights up the darkness of trying circumstances with the thought of the end, saying, "Be patient . . . until the Lord's coming" (5:7). John, exulting in present blessedness, views the end, and from the vision gathers new hope and purifying power: "Dear friends, now we are children of God. . . . We shall be like him" (1 John 3:2). Jude sees beyond the present period of growth to one of perfection: "To him that is able to keep you from falling and to present you before his glorious presence without fault" (v. 24). To this strong, courageous, and victorious outlook of the earliest saints may be added the testimony of the disciples of later centuries.

Understanding the Attitude

To this point we have made a statement only. Now let us endeavor to *understand* this attitude of the Lord and His disciples. Two statements in the New Testament are remarkable in their clear and unmistakable meaning. They will bear out all we have said. The first is contained in the words of Jesus Himself to Martha at the grave of Lazarus: "He who believes in me . . . will never die" (John 11:25, 26). The other is a statement by Paul: ". . . Our Savior Jesus Christ, who has destroyed death" (2 Timothy 1:10).

Nothing can be simpler or more forceful. Our Lord, speaking

to Martha, meant just what His words convey, that to the soul believing on Him there is no dying. To that soul death is not what it seems to humanity at large. The life that one already lives, is the very life of God and eternity, and there is no death. That is precisely the thought of Paul. The word "destroyed" literally means rendered entirely useless, robbed of its power to act.

Experiencing the Miracle

How has this been brought about, and how are the disciples of Jesus able to appropriate the stupendous miracle as an experience? On the day of Pentecost, Peter declared the fact of the resurrection of Jesus, not only to be the work of God, but to have been an absolute necessity by virtue of what Jesus was in Himself. "But God raised him up from the dead, freeing him from the agony of death, because it was impossible for death to keep its hold on him" (Acts 2:24).

So much for the reason of the Master's own view of the future. Now look at Hebrews 2:14,15: "Since the children have flesh and blood, he too shared in their humanity so that by his death he might destroy him who holds the power of death—that is the devil—and free those who all their lives were held in slavery by their fear of death." In this verse we see how through His death He has given us victory over death, and removed from us its fear. Before He left His disciples He made that great declaration, "Because I live, you also will live" (John 14:19). Therefore we are brought into the place of His victorious life, through the overcoming power of His victorious death.

If then He has abolished death, what now remains? It is still certain that these probationary days will end, this life of limitation and testing will come to a conclusion. All this changing scene will pass away. But still we do not know when death will come. How do we as disciples of Jesus differ from the crowd? Instead of death being the end, He Himself stands waiting for us and ever approaches us. Whether we are among those who are alive at the coming of the Lord, or "them that are fallen asleep," still the end of the present is Himself, for to sleep is just to be "absent from the body, at home with the Lord," not to die. To remain to His coming is just to "meet the Lord in the air." So when evening comes to the disciple and he turns his back upon the glories of the western sky and faces the east, it is not cold, and dark, and cheerless, but full of light, for the sun fills all the horizon, and so to the child of trust, "There is no night."

Disciples then are not called upon to prepare for death, but for *Him*. That hope purifies, refines, illumines all the hours with the radiance of the eternal day. We cannot fear death then, for to us all is changed. The end has become the beginning. Mystery is transformed into the vestibule of revelation. Rest from labor is entry upon highest work. At life's eventide there is the light of the eternal morning which illumines the disciple's home.

12

Only those who have been away from their earthly homes for awhile know how intensely sweet is the sense of being "at home" again.

Bear me on thy rapid wing,
Everlasting Spirit,
Where the choirs of angels sing
And the saints inherit.

—*Anonymous*

THE DISCIPLE IN GLORY

How little we know, comparatively, of the hereafter. "Life and incorruption have been brought to light" in the Gospel of Jesus, and death has been transformed from a foe to a friend, but the Revelation is characterized by its silence with regard to the future rather than by its declarations. It is as though God would not force men toward righteousness either by threatened punishment, or promised reward. Enough, however, has been said to help us to understand the terrors of being lost, and the blessedness of being saved.

As to the occupation of the disciple of Jesus in that future life, more has been said than appears on the surface. One particular passage of Scripture is constantly being half-quoted, or quoted from the Old Testament, when surely we should quote it with Paul's expository word. The prophet Isaiah wrote: "Since ancient times, no one has heard nor perceived, no eye has seen, my God besides you who acts on behalf of those who wait for him" (64:4). In quoting these verses Paul (in 1 Corinthians 2:9, 10) goes on to say that these hidden things are "revealed . . . to us by his Spirit." Yet this quotation is usually cited to prove that we *cannot* know anything of the future of the blessed.

As we pay closer attention to these passages and the correct and much more beautiful rendering of them, it will at once be discovered that there is no reference whatever either by Isaiah, or by Paul's use of Isaiah's words, to the future life. Both are referring to the wonders of the wonder-working God in the progress of events which men could not perceive or hear, save by the Spirit of God. He revealed them in due time to those who waited for Him. That men did not see the working of God in history, we need only to witness the attitude of the disciples of Jesus. Until the Holy Spirit came and illuminated their understanding, they failed to see who Jesus really was.

This is the broad principle of the teaching of the passages, and it may be applied to the case now under consideration. To the casual, unenlightened reader, the Scripture seems to say very little of the future. To the Spirit-taught person, it says far more than we can comprehend. In this chapter I want to indicate the lines of that teaching rather than attempt to exhaust the great theme. In the previous ten chapters we have dealt with the disciple in his probationary life. That is by far, and of necessity, the smaller part of his existence. Probation is of the greatest importance, but it ever presupposes something far more important stretching out beyond. The great fact of discipleship is this: it is a process of preparation of one who is not a citizen of the earth, of one whose home and place of service lie out beyond the shadows that seem to surround the vision today. In chapter 11 we saw the disciple meeting the Master at the end of probation. May we now close this study by very reverently looking within the veil, so far as it has been lifted, at the occupation and final destiny of disciples. Through all this gracious discipline they have been patiently trained by the greatest (nay, the only) Teacher of humanity.

Death Abolished

The abolishing of death makes it perfectly certain that there can be no unconscious gap in the existence of the believer. We too often speak of death as the end of life. Really, it is the crowning meeting of the disciple and his Lord. The limitations of material things, which are always in some sense a hindrance to the development of the Spirit life, are gone. In that state where "faith is lost in sight," and hope in full fruition dies, there comes a clearer, fuller consciousness. The phrases of the New Testament which describe that state give us most suggestive and valuable teaching concerning it. Let us take two of these, both from the writings of Paul.

"At Home with the Lord"

In 2 Corinthians 5:8 Paul writes, "Away from the body and at home with the Lord." The use of the phrase "at home," instead of the word "present" as in the Authorized Version, is necessary to ensure consistency of translation for the whole passage. The same word is translated "at home" in verse 6.

What a perfect and beautiful concept this is! The first consciousness of the disciple in that larger life is called, "At home." When it is analyzed, the word conveys the idea of being among one's own people. That is its true meaning. Death is that gracious transition into the condition of being perfectly at rest in the Lord's presence. In all the high spiritual aspects of our earthly life, we still have been strangers here. There, we shall be "at home." Here, our relationships have been as sojourners in tents, and strangers. Our sense of the Lord's presence, blessed as it has been, compared to what it will be then, has been only partial, and limited. There, we will be surrounded by all the conditions toward which He has led us and for which He has trained us. *There* we will first fully comprehend the meaning of much of the training of today.

O the luxury of it. Only those who have been away from their earthly homes for awhile know how intensely sweet is the sense of being "at home" again. "Home" is the one atmosphere in which there is freedom from a sense of disquietude and unrest. And yet more marvelous is the grace of it. The "at home" just beyond the shadows is "with the Lord." That I, who feared and shunned, and alas, slighted and condemned Him, am at last to be "at home" with Him, passes all telling in its evidence of His great grace.

"With Christ"

In Philippians 1:23 Paul says: "I desire to depart and be with Christ." This phrase "to depart" is undoubtedly used here in the sense of loosing a ship from its moorings. The poet, Alfred Lord Tennyson, repeated the Pauline conception when he wrote:

> "And let there be no moaning of the bar
>   When I put out to sea,
> And may there be no sadness of farewell
>   When I embark."

What then is this embarking and unloosing? Do I drift into unconsciousness for a season? No, I am with Christ.

> "I hope to see my Pilot face to face
>   When I have crossed the bar."

Note the immediateness of it. Dr. Moule says, "Not a space, but a mathematical line, divides the state of faith this side death from the state of sight that side." So then the first consciousness of the disciple in the new life is that of the Master in clear and unclouded vision.

This is the vision the Swiss preacher, César Malan, had when he wrote:

> No, no, it is not dying
>   To go unto our God.
> This gloomy earth forsaking,
> Our journey homeward taking
>   Along the starry road.
>
> No, no, it's not dying
>   To hear this gracious word,
> "Receive a Father's blessing,
> Forevermore possessing
>   The favor of thy Lord."
>
> No, no, it is not dying
>   The Shepherd's voice to know;
> His sheep He ever leadeth,
> His peaceful flock He feedeth,
>   Where living pastures grow.
>
> No, no it is not dying
>   To wear a lordly crown;
> Among God's people dwelling,
> The glorious triumph swelling
>   Of Him whose sway we own.
>
> O no, this is not dying,
>   Thou Savior of mankind!
> There, streams of love are flowing,
> No hindrance ever knowing;
>   Here, drops alone we find.

What then is the present condition and occupation of those who have departed? Between the time of their leaving this scene, and the morning of the Resurrection, there is an interval. I believe it is a time of incompleteness, for as yet they have not received their Resurrection bodies.

We have already seen that this interval is spent in a closer connection with, and a clearer vision of, Christ. The nature of their occupation is the subject of our consideration now.

In the closing words of Hebrews 11:39, 40, a great principle is declared with regard to those who have gone before. Its application by the writer of this epistle is to that great company of faithful heroes and heroines of whom he has been speaking. It may also safely be applied to all those in this Christian era who have fallen asleep or will do so: "That apart from us they should not be made perfect." In this application of the passage we are to understand that the perfecting of the disciples will only come when the Lord gathers to Himself the whole company of them. Their occupation as they wait in blessedness for the end of the age, and their gathering into the glory of the whole Church of Christ, may be described by the following line of reasoning. The Scripture itself bears testimony to this.

They are closer to Christ, and therefore their understanding of His work and service must be much clearer. This better knowledge must necessarily produce a deeper sympathy. The first propulsion of the Christ-life in the soul of the regenerate on earth was a movement of compassion toward the souls for whom He died. This resulted in an act of service on their part in some definite form or other. Now that their possession by Christ is so much more complete, it surely follows that their love for those whom He so wondrously loves, is far more intense.

Can it possibly be that this deeper love could allow them to remain inactive? Assuredly not. The things that interest and occupy Him must interest and occupy them. Thus we can only think of them as raised into a region of higher service within the same great redemptive circle in which they moved while still on the earth. It is my firm conviction that all our loved ones gone before are serving the cause of the work and purpose of God among men in a better way than they ever did in their prior life.

Does not this view light up for us many dark events in our

own lives? Those whom God has wondrously blessed here, and then suddenly called away just when we were feeling they could not be spared, have not ceased their work as we thought. No, they have been promoted to some higher place and work. With this view of the present occupation of the departed the Bible agrees: "They will rest from their labors, for their deeds will follow them" (Revelation 14:13). The immediate application is to the number of the saints who will suffer martyrdom in a subsequent era, but the truth has a present application as well. The inner teaching may perhaps best be gathered by a paraphrase, the result of a careful analysis of the words actually used: "They rest from that toil which is painful and reduces the strength, but their works, their activities, accompany them." That is to say their activity does not cease, but only that form of it which brings weariness and suffering.

So we may think of beloved servants of God: singers, teachers, preachers. Suddenly, although to all human seeming they were prematurely removed from earth and no longer involved in redemptive service, they are more than ever fully occupied in clearer light and fuller opportunity.

The Glory That Awaits

This condition of incompleteness, for them and for us, will end when "The Lord himself will come down from heaven, with a loud command, with the voice of the archangel and with the trumpet of God, and the dead in Christ will rise first. After that we who are still alive, and are left will be caught up with them in the clouds to meet the Lord in the air. And so we will be with the Lord forever" (1 Thessalonians 4:16, 17). It is there that the Church will be gathered into one complete and conscious whole, as the poet describes it:

"Some from earth, from glory some,
Severed only Till He Come."

Thus He will "present her to himself as a radiant church, without stain, or wrinkle, or any other blemish" (Ephesians 5:27).

That will be an event of the utmost importance as we look now at its bearing on the future:

Our Glorious Future

What lies ahead for the church beyond the doorway? Everything up to this point in the history of individual disciples and of the whole Church has been preparatory. It is now that the Church is ready to begin her great mission in the purpose and counsel of God. The letter to the Ephesians is specially occupied in dealing with this great and stupendous fact. The first three chapters deal with the vocation in itself, and the remainder applies the fact of that calling to every aspect of the believer while yet in this place of preparation and discipline. Let us then in concluding this study on discipleship very reverently sum up the message of in the first three chapters of that Epistle. These light up for us the great future:

Ephesians 1:18. In this verse occurs a remarkable phrase which leads the reader into the richness that follows. "The riches of his glorious inheritance in the saints." It is easy for us to understand that our inheritance is in Him. But we are at once arrested by the fact that *He* has an inheritance in *us!* And yet that is the fact. God has an inheritance in His people, and Paul's prayer is that these Ephesian Christians may have "the eyes of your heart . . . enlightened in order that you may know the hope to which he has called you, the riches of his glorious inheritance in the saints, and his incomparably great power for us who believe."

The "calling" of God is the vocation of the church. As the church fulfills that vocation, God will enter into His inheritance in her. This will be realized by the power "which he exerted in Christ when he raised him from the dead." In the paragraphs which follow, Paul proceeds to deal with the final *purpose* of God, and with the *process* by which this will be achieved. We are now interested only in that final purpose, in the fulfilling of which God will Himself possess His inheritance in His people. Now we look at the three verses which declare it.

Ephesians 2:7. "That in the coming ages he might show the incomparable riches of his grace, expressed in his kindness to us in Christ Jesus." The phrase "in the coming ages" refers to the ages of the eternal future. What future dispensations there may be, and what the movement of those ages may be, no one can tell but God Himself. Whatever these may be, the Church is to be the medium of showing forth "the riches of his grace." When those ages are to learn the love of God they are to do so by the testimony borne by the ransomed Church to His "kindness to us in Christ Jesus." Our vocation then contains within it the mission of showing to the ages yet unborn that love of God which He has exhibited to us in Jesus.

Ephesians 3:10. ". . . Now, through the church, should be made known the manifold wisdom of God to the rulers and authorities in the heavenly realms." This reveals another phase of vocation. The Church is to reveal to the unfallen intelligences, the rulers and authorities in the heavenlies the manifold wisdom of God. These shining ones have glories that far exceed anything of which we have dreamed. Their powers of comprehension are wondrously broad. Yet they will only know, through the revelation of the Church, the manifold wisdom of God in all its fullness.

Ephesians 3:21: "To him be glory in the church and in Christ Jesus throughout all generations, forever and ever!" Briefly stated then, this is the vocation of the Church, beyond all the preparation of this life, beyond that intermediate state in which some now are. In that time when the Church shall be completed and complete, its mission is to reveal the grace and wisdom of God to the beings of other dwelling places, the high unfallen ones of the heavenlies. This applies not to one age only, but to the ages of the ages as they are known only to the mind of God. In all eternity that great "Now" of God embracing our past and future, there has been no such proof of the grace of His heart and the wisdom of His workings as this: the ransoming and uplifting in spotless purity of fallen man. Those so ransomed and uplifted are to be the witnesses to the great future of intelligence concerning wondrous and overwhelming truths. What enormous possibilities this view of the Church's future opens up before us. Our finite surroundings make it impossible for us to comprehend all the infinite spaces that appear only to us as blue sky, or darkening night. What worlds are there, what high forms of pure spirits, what spaces still beyond, and what yet deeper spheres of habitable places, we do not yet know.

One's mind is bewildered at the daring of its own flight. Remember that to these worlds and these beings and these ages we are to be the messengers of the grace and wisdom and glory of God. In that view the future loses its sense of dread, and one looks on to the new opportunities for art, and music, and poetry, and above all perhaps, of preaching. These are coming to the ransomed ones when the discipline of time is merged into the fitness of eternity, with reverent and holy desire.

Someone may say that this is pure imagining. It certainly is imagination well within the limit of the possibilities of these words of the apostle Paul, who had been caught up into the third heaven and had seen things unutterable. Note how he closes this section:

Ephesians 3:20, 21: "Now to him who is able *to do* immeasurably more than all we ask or imagine, according to his power at work within us, to him be glory in the church and in Christ Jesus throughout all generations, forever and ever! Amen."

Thus, our wildest flights of thought are far short of the possibilities of what God is able "to do."

This is but a faint glimpse then of the glory of which Paul said, "I consider that our present sufferings are not worth comparing with the glory that will be revealed in us" (Romans 8:18).

But it is enough to turn our hearts with fuller consecration to that Beloved One. With a perfect knowledge of that future, too splendid yet for our comprehension, He is teaching and training us ever with that vocation in view.

How better can we close this contemplation of discipleship, in its beginning, progress and consummation, than in the words of Paul to the Ephesians, "I urge you to live a life worthy of the calling you have received" (4:1).

Additional Resources for Spiritual Growth

THE COMPANION BIBLE

Notes and appendices by E. W. Bullinger

The Most Complete One-volume Study Bible Available in the King James Version! Notes within the text give valuable insight into the original Greek and Hebrew languages. Alternate translations, explanations of figures of speech, cross-references and an introductory detailed outline of each book and chapter are among the many features which pastors, preachers, seminarians and Bible students will find helpful.

Additional helps include: 198 appendices including explanations of Hebrew words and their use, charts, parallel passages, maps, lists of proper names, calendars, timelines, etc. Notes are keyed to these indexes. Distinguishing type used for divine names and titles. Archaeological findings and historical genealogies. Factual marginal notes.

Features of both leather and deluxe hardbound editions include: King James Text, Deluxe Bible paper, Quality smyth-sewn binding, Trim size 6 1/2" x 9 1/2", 2,160 pages.

ISBN 0-8254-2203-5	2,160 pp.	Deluxe hardcover
ISBN 0-8254-2288-4	2,160 pp.	Bonded leather

HOW TO ENJOY THE BIBLE   E. W. Bullinger

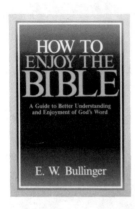

A basic introduction to the study of the Bible. E. W. Bullinger, author of *The Companion Bible, Commentary on Revelation, Witness of the Stars*, and *Number in Scripture*, brings to the reader insights on the Bible and its background. Chapter subjects include: the object and subject of the Word of God, rightly dividing the Word of God, first occurences of select words in the Scriptures, figures of speech in the Bible, and interpretation and application. *How to Enjoy the Bible* will shed light on the Bible and its content for the serious student of the Scriptures.

ISBN 0-8254-2213-2   466 pages   paperback
ISBN 0-8254-2287-6   466 pages   deluxe hardcover

THE NEW COMPACT TOPICAL BIBLE   James Inglis

The perfect Bible companion for beginning Bible students and a handy reference for pastors and teachers, *The Compact Topical Bible* is an easy-to-use treasure house of Scripture information.

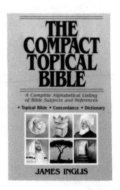

Inglis provides a complete collection of Scripture verses arranged under a comprehensive, alphabetical list of Bible subjects. All subjects found in the Bible, whether doctrinal, devotional, practical, ecclesiastical, biographical, or secular, are included.

The result is a master reference for quick and accurate Bible study, allowing the Scriptures to speak for themselves on topics from A to Z.

ISBN 0-8254-2900-5   528 pp.   paperback

THE DISCIPLER'S MANUAL   F.E. Marsh

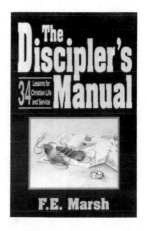

In his *Foreword* W. Herbert Scott points out the unique value of this work:

I have owned and used a copy of this work, formerly published as *Fully Furnished,* for more than forty years. Many of my best sermons had their seed in these studies. What a treasure of precious gems is found in this Spirit-prompted production! What a blessing it is that this work should be republished now to meet the need for discipling!

The child of God has a mandate from his risen Lord to love and confront the world with the issues of the Gospel, but he isn't doing it. The individual Christian is not impacting the world, because he is not equipped to perform the task his Lord has committed to him. In our day, sad to say, the roles of personal evangelism and discipling have been too often replaced by the electronic church, mass evangelism, and other modern outreach methods.

Dr. F.E. Marsh has recognized the need to spell out the elements in the discipling process. In these thirty-four studies he has set forth in a comprehensive manner all that a well-equipped servant of Christ needs to know of God's purpose and method of reaching and building men and women for God. Dr. Marsh is possessed by an uncompromising confidence in the integrity and authority of the Bible, in the perfect sufficiency of the Holy Spirit to teach, equip, lead and empower the Christian witness. In this single volume we are presented with a complete manual for discipling.

ISBN 0-8254-3283   350 pp.   paperback

DISCIPLINED BY GRACE: Studies in Christian Conduct

J. F. Strombeck

In this carefully crafted and logically developed series of studies, J.F. Strombeck explores every facet of the doctrine of grace. Included are chapters on: Grace Teaching Us, Standards of Grace Teaching, Grace Defined and Explained, By the Power of God, Grace Upon Grace, Devotion and Works, Denying Ungodliness and Works Acceptable Unto God, Worldly Lusts, God's Ways and Man's Ways, Teaching Us Godliness, Some Promptings by Grace, The Bread and the Wine, Present Your Bodies, To Do Thy Will, O God, Walk Worthy of Your Calling, The Trial of Faith, Chastening, Grace Teaches Humility, Christ Pre-eminent, The Believer's Standing and State, Looking for His Appearing

"One feature in the doctrine of grace which has been so greatly neglected is the life which is to be lived unto God after one is saved by grace. Mr. Strombeck's book, *Disciplined by Grace*, covers this ground and meets this need in a wonderful way. It should be read by every Christian. I recommend it most heartily." —Dr. Lewis Sperry Chafer

ISBN 0-8254-3776-8   160 pp.   paperback

SHALL NEVER PERISH:
Eternal Security Examined

J.F. STROMBECK

The subject of assurance is viewed from every possible standpoint and from every conceivable angle, with the result that the eternal security of the believer is thoroughly established.

"We doubt very much if a finer treatise on the assurance of salvation and the eternal security of the believer in Christ has ever been published, or could be written. The subject of assurance, which as the author says, is indispensable to a consistent, happy and fruitful Christian life, is viewed from every possible standpoint and from every conceivable angle, with the result that the eternal security of the believer is thoroughly established and triumphantly vindicated. If anyone can remain a 'doubting Thomas' after perusal of this classic work on eternal security, he must be past conviction on the subject." —*The Witness*, London

"I know nothing in print more exhaustive, direct, concise, simple, or conclusive on the subject of the eternal security of the believer than the book *Shall Never Perish*." —Dr. Lewis Sperry Chafer

ISBN 0-8254-3779-2   208 pp.   paperback

GRACE AND TRUTH: The True Relationship
Between Law and Grace   J.F. Strombeck

This in-depth yet concise study of the Gospel of John emphasizes throughout each chapter the striking contrast between law and grace, and between faith and works.

"Here is a most unusual and convincing presentation of a great Bible theme that is all too little understood by the majority of Christians....Mr. Strombeck has given us the simplest kind of study running through practically the entire Gospel of John, and has brought out in a most telling and inescapable manner a fact which probably few others have ever discovered—that in every chapter of this wonderful Gospel the striking contrast between law and grace, between faith and works, is emphasized."   —*Sunday School Times*

"I have studied, taught, and written on the doctrine of grace for many years, but gladly do I confess that new and precious treasures of truth have come to me from careful reading of this volume."

—Dr. Lewis Sperry Chafer

ISBN 0-8254-3778-4   160 pp.   paperback